all recipes™ tried & true

cookies

top 200 recipes

all recipes™

tried & true

cookies

top 200 recipes

Published by Allrecipes.com, Inc.
524 Dexter Ave. N., Seattle, WA 98109

Printed in U.S.A.
First Edition October 2001

10 9 8 7 6 5 4 3 2 1

ISBN 0-9711-7231-5

EDITOR: Tim Hunt
SENIOR RECIPE EDITOR: Syd Carter
SENIOR FOOD EDITOR: Jennifer Anderson
SENIOR PRODUCTION MANAGER: Liz Rogers
RECIPE EDITORS: Emily Brune, Britt Swearingen, Richard Kozel
CREATIVE DIRECTION: Yann Oehl
DESIGN: Jeff Cummings

dedication

This book is dedicated to all mothers and
grandmothers. The most important
ingredient in the cookies you gave us
was the love you baked into them.

acknowledgments

The book you are holding is a community cookbook. The recipes within come from the community of cooks who gather online at Allrecipes.com. It is the members of this community, first and foremost, who we would like to thank — anyone who has shared, reviewed, requested, or tried an Allrecipes recipe. The success of the Allrecipes community resides in your experience, enthusiasm, and generosity.

In addition, a huge debt of thanks is owed to the staff of Allrecipes — the people who have dedicated themselves to building a helpful, supportive environment for our community.

table of contents

cookies — the great tradition

Cookies evoke our earliest memories of home baking: peering over the counter as each wonderful ingredient is added to the mixing bowl, impatiently eyeing the baking sheets as they fill with ranks of dough, watching that magical transformation through the oven door as the house fills with the sweet aroma of baking. Then comes the long-awaited moment — the indescribable burst of pleasure as the first just-barely-cooled bite of cookie melts into flavor in our hungry mouths. These memories return with each batch we bake and are the reason that cookies have come to symbolize home, joy, caring, sharing, and love.

Cookie baking is one of the oldest and most widespread of culinary traditions. The word "cookie" evolved from the Dutch word *koekje*, which means "little cake." Every culture has its tradition of "little cakes," ranging from Scottish shortbread to Chinese moon cakes, Italian biscotti to American chocolate chip cookies. Cookies come in all shapes, sizes, flavors, and textures, but they do have some things in common: they're small enough to hold in your hand and easy enough for anyone to bake at home. Cookies are easy to carry and hand out — they're built for sharing. They've been a staple feature of feasts and festivals since ancient times, but are quick and easy enough for everyday munching.

Like all great traditions, cookie baking is handed down from generation to generation — each adding a little of its own creativity and sharing new ideas from other traditions. In 1997 we built an Internet web site called CookieRecipe.com where folks could go online to find and share cookie recipes. The web site was instantly popular; more and more recipes were added, and it eventually blossomed into the Allrecipes.com web site millions of people use today. All of the recipes you'll find in this cookbook were contributed by users and represent the highest rated recipes chosen from over 3000 cookies.

In the pages that follow, we've also included all the tips and tricks you need to become a cookie-baking genius — how to fine-tune your recipes to get the results you want; whether crispy or chewy, puffy or flat, plain or fanciful. Cookies are just too wonderful to keep to yourself, so we've included some quick ideas for gift-giving, mailing cookies safely, and organizing the best cookie exchange party ever! Keep in mind that the art of cookie baking is only limited by your imagination. And always remember that cookies are for sharing.

making cookies — fine-tuning for your taste

building the perfect cookie

Some people like their cookies crisp and delicate. Others prefer a chewy cookie with a thickness that they can sink their teeth into. The exact same recipe can bake up into two completely different cookies; the flavor will be the same but the texture will be different. How, you ask? The reasons all lie within the variables of ingredients, mixing technique, temperature, and equipment.

ingredients

Fats: the fats most often used in cookies are butter, margarine, shortening, and oil. They play a big part in determining whether your cookie spreads out into a thin mass on the cookie sheet or retains its original shape. Shortening, margarine, and oils are fairly heat-stable — they will help cookies keep their original unbaked shape. Butter melts at a much lower temperature than the other solid fats, so cookies made with butter tend to spread out. The amount of fat also affects the cookies: more fat yields flatter, chewier, crispier cookies; less fat produces puffier, more cake-like cookies.

Flour: flours with a high protein content (like all-purpose or bread flour) will produce cookies that are flatter, darker, and crisper than those made with cake or pastry flour.

Leavening: the difference between the two most common forms of leavening — baking powder and baking soda — is this: baking powder contains an acidic ingredient (cream of tartar) and baking soda does not. Baking powder will tend to produce lighter-colored and puffier cookies than baking soda.

Sugars: white sugar will make a crispier cookies than brown sugar or honey. Cookies made from brown sugar will actually absorb moisture as they stand, giving them a chewy texture. If you reduce the amount of sugar called for in a cookie recipe, the baked cookies will tend to be puffier.

Eggs and liquids: eggs will help to promote puffiness, while just a tablespoon or two of water (or other liquid) will help your cookies spread into flatter, crisper rounds. Egg yolks will make cookies moist, whereas egg whites lend a drier texture.

mixing technique

The most important step in cookie mixing is creaming. This is the step where the fat and the sugar are beaten, mixed, and whipped together until they are light-colored, fluffy, and smooth. This helps to incorporate air into the batter, which you need for the leavening to work. Another important tip is not to overmix the dough; do so, and you'll truly understand the meaning of "tough cookies!" Once you mix together the wet and dry ingredients, stir until just combined.

temperature

The first step in cookie baking is always to preheat the oven. Skip it and your first batch will be a disaster. Chilled cookie dough will hold its shape during baking and produce a slightly puffier cookie, room temperature dough will spread and flatten out while baking. If you want your cookies to be chewy, the trick is to underbake them slightly. If you want them to be crispy, bake them a little longer. Keep your eye on the clock! One minute can make a huge difference in the short life of a baking cookie, so get yourself a good timer and an accurate oven thermometer. Keep an especially watchful eye until you've become intimately acquainted with the quirks of your oven, your cookie sheets, and your dough — you'll soon learn the exact time and temperature required to launch your cookies to the zenith of perfection!

equipment

A good baking sheet can make a big difference. Super-thin baking sheets will cause the bottoms of the cookies to bake faster, sometimes burning their undersides. Insulated, or air-cushion baking sheets allow air-flow under the cookie-baking surface, reducing hotspots and resulting in perfect cookies all across the sheet, not just in the middle. However, while you get consistent heat throughout the sheet, insulated sheets don't always reach the proper temperature. You may want to run your oven a few degrees hotter when using these sheets, but give them a test run at the temperature indicated in the recipe. Cookies baked on insulated sheets will be puffier, so if you want flat, crisp cookies, your best bet is to use the standard medium-thick baking sheets that are widely available.

Greasing your cookie sheets before baking will cause the cookies to spread out more, resulting in a thinner, crisper cookie. But, if you don't grease the sheets you run the risk of the cookies sticking and ruining the batch. A good and fairly inexpensive solution to this is parchment paper. This paper is coated on each side, usually with a light coating of food-grade silicone, and comes on a roll like wax paper. Just tear off a sheet of parchment and line the baking sheet. Your cookies will lift off with ease. Another option is reusable silicone pan liners. These are sturdy, flexible sheets that you can use again and again with perfect, no-burn, no-stick results every time.

quick reference

Flat cookies: use butter and all-purpose flour or bread flour, and increase the sugar content slightly. Add a bit of liquid to your recipe and bring the dough to room temperature before baking.

Puffy cookies: use shortening or margarine and cut back on the fat, add an egg, reduce the sugar, use cake flour or pastry flour, use baking powder instead of baking soda, refrigerate the dough before baking.

Chewy cookies: remove the cookies a few minutes before they are done, while the edges are golden but the middle still looks slightly doughy. Use brown sugar or honey as a sweetener, replace each whole egg with two egg yolks.

Crispy cookies: bake your cookies a few minutes longer than suggested and immediately remove them to wire racks to cool. Use all butter and a high ratio of white sugar, as well as all-purpose or bread flour.

making your cookies beautiful

You can quickly make any batch of cookies extra-special with one of these easy decorating techniques.

frostings and icings

The most popular and versatile technique for decorating cookies is to frost or ice them. The simplest types of cookie icing are made with confectioners' sugar, butter, and milk or water. These icings have a somewhat softer texture than royal icings — which are made with confectioners' sugar, egg whites, and lemon juice. Royal icings dry to a very hard, crunchy finish. They are great for gluing gingerbread houses, but not quite as tasty as fat-based icings.

Flavored extracts, such as vanilla, lemon, orange, or almond, can be added for variety. Juice can also be substituted for the liquid in a recipe. It's fun to make a different flavor for each color. The icing can be colored using liquid food coloring, but for brighter colors, paste food coloring works best. To make the color more even, start by mixing the color into about one tablespoon of icing, then blend that into the rest of the icing. Frosting can easily be thinned to the desired consistency by adding liquid, such as milk, juice, or water. For a smooth, glossy finish, warm the icing slightly in the microwave or in a bowl over a pan of simmering water. Be sure to stir frequently so that a crust does not form on top.

spread the sweetness

Frosting can be applied using a pastry brush or by simply dipping the cookies into the mixture. Set freshly frosted cookies onto a tray or wax paper to dry. Once the first coat of frosting sets, you can pipe another color of frosting over the top to add details such as stripes, spirals, faces, or names. A plastic baggie with the corner cut off works well, as do the disposable plastic pastry bags that can be purchased at cake-decorating supply or craft stores. Press pieces of candy into the frosting before it hardens or sprinkle the cookies with different colors of sugar. For an elegant touch, try edible glitter or gold dust.

chocolate

A dip in chocolate makes any cookie irresistible. Darker chocolates need to be tempered to keep them shiny and firm. The best way to get around this step is to buy a type of chocolate called "coating chocolate," which usually comes in the shape of small discs for more convenient melting (white coating chocolate is also known as "almond bark"). Coating chocolate is specially designed to hold a nice shine without tempering, but may not taste as quite as chocolaty as the regular semi-sweet variety. If you'd like to learn more about tempering chocolate, visit us at Allrecipes.com and we'll walk you through the process! Go to: **http://allrecipes.com/cb/kh/dessert/chocolate/**

Decorating with chocolate is easy, but it helps to be organized. First, put your chocolate into a heatproof bowl and set this on top of a pan of simmering water. Chocolate burns very easily and cannot be melted directly on the stovetop. A microwave oven also works well, just be sure to stir every 15 seconds or so.

While the chocolate is melting, arrange your workspace so that the cookies you wish to dip are on one side and a couple of cookie sheets lined with parchment or wax paper are on the other side. When most of the chocolate is melted, remove from the heat and stir until smooth. This will melt it the rest of the way and will also cool it a bit so that you do not burn your hands.

Dip cookies halfway into the chocolate, then scrape the excess off the bottom using your finger or the side of the bowl. Give the cookie a gentle shake and once again scrape off the excess chocolate. Place the cookies onto the wax paper, starting at the farthest end and working inward.

If you like nuts, dip one end of each cookie into finely chopped pistachios or peanuts while the chocolate is still wet. Try dipping one half of each cookie in dark chocolate, and the other half in white. Striping also lends an elegant touch to the cookies: simply spoon chocolate into a plastic bag, snipping off one corner and drizzling the chocolate through the hole.

decorating before baking

If you want great-looking cookies but don't want to make an all-day production out of it, there are a few ways to add a special touch before the cookies are even baked. One method is to roll them in colored sugar, finely chopped nuts, coconut, sesame seeds, or sprinkles before baking. Even a light dusting of confectioners' sugar or cocoa powder will give any cookies an elegant finish. Dust the cookies again right before serving to freshen their appearance.

sharing the love — it's better to give....

cookie mixes

Homemade cookie and brownie mixes (a pre-measured collection of all of the dry ingredients in a recipe), make great gifts. There are two ways to put these together: either you can layer the ingredients in a clear glass jar so that each layer is distinct, or you can sift everything together first (a recipe using either method can easily be adapted to the other.) Keep in mind that if you're going for the layered look, the ingredients need to have different colors and textures for an attractive appearance.

All of the cookie mix recipes in this cookbook will fit into a 1-quart or 1-liter size wide-mouth canning jar as long as you pack the ingredients tightly. (One quart equals 4 cups; one liter equals just over 4 cups.) After placing one ingredient in the jar, press it down using a utensil with a fairly wide, flat bottom (a long-handled tart tamper is perfect). When layering, keep in mind that white sugar, confectioners' sugar, and flour tend to seep down into chunky layered items (like colored candies, chocolate chips, nuts, etc.) It's better to layer the fine ingredients at the bottom.

After you've filled the jars, cover the lids with festive fabric, draw on them with puffy paint, or tie them with ribbons or raffia. One way to get around the problem of finding just the right jar is to use heavy-duty plastic bags. Once you've filled the plastic bags with the mix, you can place them in a decorative tin, cookie jar, cloth-lined basket, or beautiful mixing bowl. You can even create an entire baking kit! Along with the mix, be sure to include a cookie sheet, measuring spoons, cups, timer, and oven thermometer.

Remember to attach a card with the instructions on how to finish the recipe. It's also a good idea to include the amounts of the dry ingredients you used — that way the recipient can make the gift again and again. If stored in a cool, dry, dark place, your gift can last up to six months.

mailing cookies

Everyone loves to get cookies in the mail. Here are some tips to guarantee that your home-baked love survives the trip.

choosing cookies to mail

Cookies that have a crunchy or hard texture such as biscotti, Mexican wedding cakes, crisps, springerle, and shortbreads make excellent choices for mail delivery. Cookies that have a slightly chewy texture, like chocolate chip, oatmeal-raisin, snickerdoodles, and white-chocolate cranberry cookies also ship well. However, these cookies tend to dry out if they are in the mail for more than a week, so consider shipping them express. Macaroons and pignoli mail beautifully; their chewy, moist texture only seems to improve after they've aged a few days. Dense bar cookies such as fudge brownies, blondies, or peanut butter bars also mail well. Be sure to individually wrap each bar with plastic wrap to keep that moist, gooey, dense texture from drying out.

We recommend that you do not mail cookies with custard-like fillings or toppings, or any cookie that requires refrigeration, including cheesecake bars or Nanaimo bars. The custard could spoil, making a very unwelcome gift. Other cookies that are better left at home include those with delicate, cake-like textures such as madeleines, as well as cut-out cookies with fragile features or odd shapes.

packing do's and don'ts

Pack cookies in a sturdy tin or airtight container. Place a piece of bubble wrap in the bottom of the container, then line with parchment paper or cellophane, leaving enough to tuck over the top once the container is fully packed. Place one layer of cookies in the container and cover with parchment paper. Arrange another layer of cookies, followed with more parchment paper, and continue this layering technique until the container is full. Tuck the cellophane or parchment paper over the top, then add another piece of bubble wrap, and seal your container.

Don't pack crisp and soft cookies together. The moisture from the soft cookies will seep into the crisp cookies, making them lose their delightful crunch. Don't overstuff your container, or your cookies may arrive damaged. Likewise, don't under-pack your container — the cookies should fit snugly. If you have too much space, crumple up a bit of tissue paper to fill the holes.

Place the cookie-filled, snugly-packed container in a heavy-duty cardboard box that's large enough to allow a two- to three-inch cushion between the tin and the wall of the outside box. Place a layer of shipping peanuts, air-popped popcorn, or crumpled paper on the bottom of the box. Set the cookie tin on this bottom layer and then fill in the sides and top with more packing materials. Tape the shipping box tightly shut and seal with a kiss!

cookie exchange parties

A cookie exchange party makes it possible for everyone who participates to take home a gigantic assortment of homemade cookies to serve during the holidays with minimal effort.

On your party invitations, ask each person to bring a big batch of cookies (estimate one dozen multiplied by the total number of guests, plus an extra dozen for sampling), a stack of recipe cards, and cookie containers for the trip home. Make sure that your guests understand that the cookies they bring must be homemade and easily transportable. That means no soft icings and no refrigerator cookies, because they are likely to get, well, *smooshed* in transit. Since variety is the name of the game, ask everyone to RSVP and tell you what kind of cookie they plan to bring.

When everyone arrives, organize the cookies and recipe cards buffet-style on a table. Allow some time for socializing and snacking. You might even ask each guest to tell a story about his or her cookie. It could be a story about the cookie's origin, where the cook learned the recipe, or how the particular batch of cookies was made. When story time draws to a close, let the swapping begin!

If you'd like to turn your party into an opportunity to give a little something to your community, share the sweet rewards of your cookie exchange with local shelters or youth organizations. Ask your guests to bring disposable cookie containers, festive ribbons, and small cards with them. Write short messages of caring and encouragement, and have everyone sign their names before attaching the cards and ribbons to the parcels of assorted home-baked treats.

recipe tips

variations on a theme

You may wonder why we offer more than one recipe for some cookies, such as chocolate chip or gingerbread. Don't worry — these are far from being duplicate recipes! Some cookies are so popular that our community members share multiple versions of them. In fact, when you visit Allrecipes.com, you'll find that we have dozens of variations for many of your favorite recipes. As we post new recipes, we'll add a Roman numeral to the title to distinguish it (i.e., the "Monster Cookies II" recipe which appears in this book). You'll find there are lots of different ways to approach the old standbys, and in this book, you can enjoy your next batch of chocolate chippers with the crunch of macadamia nuts, or the hearty chewiness of oats, or you can concentrate your baking efforts on the pure, unadorned, crisp-on-the-edges, soft-in-the-middle, chocolate chip cookie. Come see us at Allrecipes.com to explore new takes on all your old favorites.

about the recipes

Half the fun of an Allrecipes recipe is the story behind it — each of our recipes has comments submitted by the contributor to help explain how the recipe came about, what it's like, or how they use it. As the editors of the Allrecipes cookbooks (both online and in print), the staff works hard to preserve the character of the contributed recipe, but also strives to ensure consistency, accuracy, and completeness in the published version and throughout the collection.

all in the timing

At the top right corner of every recipe in the book you'll find "Preparation," "Cooking," and "Total" times. These are approximate! Depending on the power of your mixer, whether or not you remembered to pre-soften the butter, how hot your oven gets, your altitude, how much time you have to spend chasing people who are trying to run off with handfuls of cookie dough, or any number of other factors, you may find that it takes less or more time than we've estimated. The Preparation time tells you how long it takes to make the cookie dough, and, if applicable, to roll it out, cut it, shape it, roll it in sugar, or flatten it with a fork. The Cooking time is about how long it takes to bake one batch of cookies. The Total time is an estimate of how long it will take you between opening the book and lifting the very last cookie off the pan. To reach the Total number, we added up the Preparation time, plus the length of time it will take to bake ALL of the cookies (we assume that most ovens can accommodate two dozen cookies), plus any additional time to chill the dough and decorate. Whew!

need help? we're here for you!

Need more information about an unfamiliar ingredient or baking term, general cooking information, or difficult techniques? We've got a whole section at Allrecipes.com dedicated to giving you all the assistance you need. In our "Cooking Basics" section, you can search for thousands of kitchen terms, follow photo-filled step-by-step tutorials to learn important baking skills, and browse or search hundreds of articles that will help you decide what to make and teach you how to make it. You can access the Cooking Basics section at Allrecipes. **http://allrecipes.com/cb/**

beyond the book

Each of the recipes in this book can be accessed at Allrecipes.com. The online versions have some handy, whiz-bang features we didn't manage to squeeze into this book. If you'd like to adjust the number of servings for a recipe, view detailed nutritional information, convert the measurements to metric, or email a copy to a friend, it's all just a click away. We've created a special place on Allrecipes.com where you can find any recipe in this book simply by entering its page number. Check it out! **http://allrecipes.com/tnt/cookies/page.asp**

your two cents

Once you try a recipe in this book, you can tell the rest of the world all about it! First, locate the recipe on Allrecipes.com (see above). Next, click on the link that says "Add to Recipe Box" (below the recipe's description). Then, follow the instructions to set up a free recipe box of your own. Once you've added the recipe to your box, you can rate it on a scale of one to five stars and share your comments with the millions of other people who use the site. Come tell us what you think!

tried and true

If you'd like to find out more about this book, the recipes, and other Allrecipes "tried and true" cookbooks, join us online at **http://allrecipes.com/tnt/** or send us an email at **tnt@allrecipes.com**.

chocolate & chocolate chip

Ahhh…the mysterious, sultry spell that chocolate casts: who can resist? Some prefer chocolate cookies, silky-smooth and rich with flavor — elegant and intense. Many argue that the pinnacle of the cookie-baking art is represented by the union of brown-sugar cookie dough studded with morsels of semi-sweet chocolate — the quintessential chocolate chip cookie. Can't decide? Try some chocolate-chocolate chippers!

Chewy Chocolate Cookies II

Submitted by: **Lois Wells**

Makes: 4 dozen

Preparation: 15 minutes

Cooking: 9 minutes

Total: 45 minutes

"Delicious cookies that taste like brownies."

INGREDIENTS

1¼ cups margarine, softened

2 cups white sugar

2 eggs

2 teaspoons vanilla extract

2 cups all-purpose flour

¾ cup unsweetened cocoa powder

1 teaspoon baking soda

⅛ teaspoon salt

1 cup chopped walnuts

DIRECTIONS

1. Preheat oven to 350°F (175°C).

2. In a large bowl, cream together margarine and sugar until smooth. Beat in eggs one at a time, then stir in the vanilla. Combine flour, cocoa, baking soda, and salt; stir into the creamed mixture until just blended. Mix in walnuts. Drop by spoonfuls onto ungreased cookie sheets.

3. Bake for 8 to 10 minutes in the preheated oven. Cool for a couple of minutes on the cookie sheet before transferring to wire racks to cool completely.

Ultimate Double Chocolate Cookies

Submitted by: **Carol P.**

Makes: 3½ dozen

Preparation: 25 minutes

Cooking: 10 minutes

Total: 1 hour 40 minutes

"A chocolate cookie with the intensity of hot fudge sauce. THIS IS THE BEST CHOCOLATE COOKIE!!! Thick And Chewy!"

INGREDIENTS

1 pound semisweet chocolate, chopped

2 cups all-purpose flour

½ cup Dutch process cocoa powder

2 teaspoons baking powder

1 teaspoon salt

10 tablespoons unsalted butter

1½ cups packed brown sugar

½ cup white sugar

4 eggs

2 teaspoons instant coffee granules

2 teaspoons vanilla extract

DIRECTIONS

1. Melt chocolate over a double boiler or in the microwave, stirring occasionally until smooth. Sift together flour, cocoa, baking powder, and salt; set aside.

2. In a medium bowl, cream butter with white sugar and brown sugar until smooth. Beat in eggs one at a time, then stir in coffee crystals and vanilla until well blended. Stir in melted chocolate. Using a wooden spoon, stir in the dry ingredients just until everything comes together. Cover, and let stand for 35 minutes so the chocolate can set up.

3. Preheat the oven to 350°F (175°C). Line two cookie sheets with parchment paper. Roll dough into walnut sized balls, or drop by rounded tablespoonfuls onto the prepared cookie sheets, leaving 2 inches between cookies.

4. Bake for 8 to 10 minutes in the preheated oven. Cookies will be set, but the centers will still be very soft because of the chocolate. Allow cookies to cool on the baking sheets for 10 minutes before transferring to wire racks to cool completely.

Cappuccino Flats

Submitted by: **Michele Prenovost**

Makes: 55 cookies

Preparation: 15 minutes

Cooking: 12 minutes

Total: 6 hours 50 minutes

"A sliced cookie that has a nice chocolate, cinnamon and coffee taste."

INGREDIENTS

2 cups all-purpose flour

1 teaspoon ground cinnamon

1/4 teaspoon salt

1/2 cup shortening

1/2 cup butter

1/2 cup white sugar

1/2 cup packed brown sugar

1 tablespoon instant coffee granules, dissolved in 1 teaspoon water

2 (1 ounce) squares unsweetened chocolate, melted

1 egg

1 1/2 cups semisweet chocolate chips

3 tablespoons shortening

DIRECTIONS

1. In a medium bowl, stir together flour, cinnamon, and salt.

2. In a large bowl, cream together 1/2 cup shortening, butter, white sugar, and brown sugar until light and fluffy. Beat in coffee mixture, melted chocolate, and egg. Stir in the flour mixture. Cover, and chill for 1 hour, or until dough is no longer sticky. Shape dough into two rolls, 7 inches long. Wrap, and chill for at least 6 hours.

3. Preheat the oven to 350°F (175°C). Cut rolls into 1/4 inch thick slices. Place on ungreased cookie sheets.

4. Bake for 10 to 12 minutes in preheated oven. Remove from baking sheets to cool on wire racks.

5. In a small heavy saucepan over low heat, melt semisweet chocolate chips and 3 tablespoons shortening, stirring occasionally until smooth. Remove from heat. Dip half of each cookie into chocolate mixture. Place on waxed paper until the chocolate is set.

Chocolate Crinkles II

Submitted by: **Ingrid**

"Chocolate cookies coated in confectioners' sugar... very good!"

INGREDIENTS

1 cup unsweetened cocoa powder

2 cups white sugar

1/2 cup vegetable oil

4 eggs

2 teaspoons vanilla extract

2 cups all-purpose flour

2 teaspoons baking powder

1/2 teaspoon salt

1/2 cup confectioners' sugar

DIRECTIONS

1. In a medium bowl, mix together cocoa, white sugar, and vegetable oil. Beat in eggs one at a time, then stir in the vanilla. Combine the flour, baking powder, and salt; stir into the cocoa mixture. Cover dough, and chill for at least 4 hours.

2. Preheat oven to 350°F (175°C). Line cookie sheets with parchment paper. Roll dough into one inch balls. I like to use a number 50 size scoop. Coat each ball in confectioners' sugar before placing onto prepared cookie sheets.

3. Bake in preheated oven for 10 to 12 minutes. Let stand on the cookie sheet for a minute before transferring to wire racks to cool.

Chocolate Snowballs

Submitted by: **Crystal**

Makes: 6 dozen

Preparation: 15 minutes

Cooking: 20 minutes

Total: 3 hours 15 minutes

"If you like Russian Teacakes and chocolate, you'll love these tasty, tender cookies!"

INGREDIENTS

1¼ cups butter

⅔ cup white sugar

1 teaspoon vanilla extract

2 cups all-purpose flour

⅛ teaspoon salt

½ cup unsweetened cocoa powder

2 cups chopped pecans

½ cup confectioners' sugar for decoration

DIRECTIONS

1. In a medium bowl, cream butter and sugar until light and fluffy. Stir in the vanilla. Sift together the flour, salt, and cocoa; stir into the creamed mixture. Mix in the pecans until well blended. Cover, and chill for at least 2 hours.

2. Preheat oven to 350°F (175°C). Roll chilled dough into 1 inch balls. Place on ungreased cookie sheets about 2 inches apart.

3. Bake for 20 minutes in preheated oven. Roll in confectioners' sugar when cooled.

Austrian Chocolate Balls

Submitted by: **Cindy Becker**

Makes: 3 dozen

Preparation: 15 minutes

Cooking: 10 minutes

Total: 45 minutes

"Delicate dark chocolate balls topped with a rich dark chocolate glaze."

INGREDIENTS

2 (1 ounce) squares unsweetened chocolate

⅓ cup butter

1 cup white sugar

1 egg

1 egg yolk

½ teaspoon almond extract

1⅓ cups all-purpose flour

½ cup finely chopped walnuts

1 (1 ounce) square unsweetened chocolate

1 tablespoon butter

¼ teaspoon vanilla extract

1 cup confectioners' sugar

3 tablespoons milk

DIRECTIONS

1. In a small saucepan over low heat, melt 2 squares of chocolate with ⅓ cup of butter. Stir frequently until melted; remove from heat, and set aside to cool. Preheat oven to 350°F (175°C).

2. In a medium bowl, mix sugar, egg, egg yolk, and almond extract until light and fluffy. Stir in the melted chocolate. Combine flour and walnuts, and stir into the batter until just combined. Shape dough into ¾ inch balls, and place them 1 inch apart on ungreased cookie sheets. If the dough is too sticky, refrigerate for 30 minutes before forming balls.

3. Bake in the preheated oven for 8 to 12 minutes, or until firm to the touch. Transfer to wire racks immediately, and set aside to cool.

4. In a small saucepan over low heat, melt 1 square of chocolate and 1 tablespoon butter together, stirring frequently until smooth. Remove from heat, and stir in vanilla and confectioners' sugar until well blended. Beat in the milk one tablespoon at a time until the glaze is of the desired consistency. Dip the tops of the cookies into the glaze, and allow to dry completely before storing in an airtight container.

Chocolate Balls

Submitted by: **Cynthia Escalante**

Makes: 3 dozen

Preparation: 20 minutes

Total: 35 minutes

"This is a peanut butter and graham cracker, chocolate covered treat. My mother made these to send to friends and relatives at Christmas time."

INGREDIENTS

1 cup peanut butter

3/4 cup confectioners' sugar

1 cup graham cracker crumbs

2 cups semisweet chocolate chips

3 (1 ounce) squares semisweet chocolate, chopped

1 tablespoon shortening

DIRECTIONS

1. In a medium bowl, mix together the peanut butter and confectioners' sugar until smooth. Stir in graham cracker crumbs until well blended. Form the dough into 1 inch balls by rolling in your hands, or by using a cookie scoop.

2. Melt the semisweet chocolate chips, semisweet chocolate squares, and the shortening in the top half of a double boiler. Use a fork to dip the balls into the melted chocolate, and place on wax paper to cool until set.

Coconut Bon Bons

Submitted by: **Tamme**

Makes: 3 dozen

Preparation: 30 minutes

Cooking: 5 minutes

Total: 2 hours 5 minutes

"These little balls of joy are perfect for any occasion."

INGREDIENTS

¼ cup butter

1 pound confectioners' sugar

1 cup sweetened condensed milk

2 cups flaked coconut

9 (1 ounce) squares semisweet chocolate

2 tablespoons shortening

DIRECTIONS

1. In a medium bowl, mix together butter, confectioners' sugar, and sweetened condensed milk. Mix in the coconut. Roll dough into 1 inch balls, and refrigerate until set, about 1 hour.

2. Melt chocolate and shortening over a double boiler, stirring occasionally until smooth. Remove from heat when melted, and stir to make sure the shortening is fully incorporated. Use toothpicks to hold the balls while dipping in the chocolate. Set on wax paper to dry.

Chocolate Swirls

Submitted by: **Ann**

Makes: 4 dozen

Preparation: 20 minutes

Cooking: 12 minutes

Total: 1 hour

"If you love chocolate and cream cheese, you'll love these cookies. At little goes a long way. Make them small, they do not spread."

INGREDIENTS

½ cup butter, softened

½ cup packed brown sugar

½ cup white sugar

1 (3 ounce) package cream cheese

1 egg

1 teaspoon vanilla extract

2 cups all-purpose flour

½ teaspoon baking powder

¼ teaspoon salt

1 cup semisweet chocolate chips, melted

DIRECTIONS

1. Preheat oven to 350°F (175°C).

2. In large bowl, cream together butter, brown sugar, and white sugar until smooth. Beat in cream cheese, egg, and vanilla. Combine flour, baking powder, and salt; mix into creamed mixture to form a soft dough. Fold in the melted chocolate until the dough is just marbled. Do not over mix. Drop dough by heaping teaspoons onto ungreased cookie sheets. Cookies should be about 2 inches apart.

3. Bake for 10 to 12 minutes in the preheated oven, or until edges are light golden brown. Cool completely before storing.

Chewy Chocolate Peanut Butter Chip Cookies

Submitted by: **Karen Rose**

"Chocolate cookies with peanut butter chips instead of chocolate chips."

INGREDIENTS

1½ cups butter, melted

2 cups white sugar

2 eggs

1 teaspoon vanilla extract

2 cups all-purpose flour

¾ cup unsweetened cocoa powder

1 teaspoon baking soda

½ teaspoon salt

2 cups peanut butter chips

DIRECTIONS

1. Preheat oven to 350°F (175°C).

2. In a large bowl, mix together butter and sugar. Beat in eggs and vanilla. Combine flour, cocoa, baking soda, and salt; gradually stir into the butter mixture. Mix in peanut butter chips. Drop by rounded teaspoons onto ungreased cookie sheets.

3. Bake 8 to 10 minutes in preheated oven. Cool for 1 minute before placing on wire racks to cool completely.

Devil's Food Peanut Butter Chip Cookies

Submitted by: **Deanna Storz**

Makes: 5 dozen

Preparation: 10 minutes

Cooking: 12 minutes

Total: 45 minutes

"This easy recipe makes the best cookies. I started making these at Christmas about 10 years ago, and now I think my family would disown me if I did not make them."

INGREDIENTS

2 eggs

1 teaspoon vanilla extract

2/3 cup shortening

1 (18.25 ounce) package devil's food cake mix

2 cups peanut butter chips

DIRECTIONS

1. Preheat oven to 375°F (190°C).

2. In a medium bowl, beat the eggs, vanilla, and shortening with ½ of the cake mix until light and fluffy. Mix in the remaining cake mix and the peanut butter chips. Drop dough by rounded teaspoonfuls 2 inches apart onto ungreased cookie sheets.

3. Bake for 10 to 12 minutes in preheated oven. Remove from cookie sheets to cool on wire racks.

Chocolate Chip Peppermint Cookies

Submitted by: **Courtney**

Makes: 30 cookies

Preparation: 15 minutes

Cooking: 12 minutes

Total: 50 minutes

"A chocolaty chocolate chip cookie, with peppermint flavoring. This is for kids or adults (I'm a 10 year old.) They taste best when they're still hot."

INGREDIENTS

3/4 cup butter

1/2 cup white sugar

1/2 cup packed brown sugar

1 egg

1 teaspoon vanilla extract

1 teaspoon peppermint extract

1 1/2 cups all-purpose flour

1/4 cup unsweetened cocoa powder

1 teaspoon baking soda

1/4 teaspoon salt

1 cup semisweet chocolate chips

DIRECTIONS

1. Preheat oven to 350°F (175°C). Grease cookie sheets.

2. In a large bowl, cream together butter, white sugar, and brown sugar until light and fluffy. Beat in egg, then stir in vanilla and peppermint extracts. Combine flour, cocoa powder, baking soda, and salt; gradually stir into the creamed mixture. Mix in the chocolate chips. Drop by rounded spoonfuls onto the prepared cookie sheets.

3. Bake for 12 to 15 minutes in the preheated oven. Allow cookies to cool on cookie sheets for 5 minutes before transferring to a wire rack to cool completely.

Peppermint Patty Surprise

Submitted by: **Linda Carroll**

Makes: 3 dozen

Preparation: 25 minutes

Cooking: 12 minutes

Total: 1 hour

"A chocolaty, minty cookie dough with a surprise peppermint patty inside!"

INGREDIENTS

2 cups mint chocolate chips, divided

1/2 cup butter

1 cup white sugar

2 egg

1 1/2 teaspoons vanilla extract

1 1/2 cups all-purpose flour

1 1/2 teaspoons baking powder

1/4 teaspoon salt

27 mini peppermint patties, quartered

2/3 cup confectioners' sugar for rolling

DIRECTIONS

1. Preheat oven to 350°(175°C). In a microwave oven, melt 1 cup mint chocolate chips, stirring frequently until smooth; set aside to cool.

2. In a large bowl, cream butter and sugar until smooth. Stir in the melted chocolate, eggs, and vanilla. Blend in flour, baking powder, and salt. Then mix in the remaining mint chocolate chips.

3. Wrap about 1 tablespoon of dough around each peppermint patty quarter. Roll balls in confectioners' sugar, and place 1½ inches apart on the cookie sheet.

4. Bake for 10 to 12 minutes in preheated oven. Roll warm cookies in confectioners' sugar again.

Caramel Filled Chocolate Cookies

Submitted by: **Lisa**

Makes: 4 dozen

Preparation: 20 minutes

Cooking: 10 minutes

Total: 3 hours

"Chocolate cookie dough is wrapped around caramel filled chocolate candies. We have these at Christmas time each year. They are delicious! Hope you enjoy them too."

INGREDIENTS

1 cup butter, softened

1 cup white sugar

1 cup packed brown sugar

2 eggs

2 teaspoons vanilla extract

2¼ cups all-purpose flour

1 teaspoon baking soda

¾ cup unsweetened cocoa powder

1 cup chopped walnuts

1 tablespoon white sugar

48 chocolate-covered caramel candies

DIRECTIONS

1. Beat butter until creamy. Gradually beat in white sugar and brown sugar. Beat in eggs and vanilla. Combine flour, baking soda, and cocoa. Gradually add to butter mixture, beating well. Stir in ½ cup walnuts. Cover and chill at least 2 hours.

2. Preheat oven to 375°F (190°C).

3. Combine remaining ½ cup nuts with the 1 tablespoon sugar. Divide the dough into 4 parts. Work with one part at a time, leaving the remainder in the refrigerator until needed. Divide each part into 12 pieces. Quickly press each piece of dough around a chocolate covered caramel. Roll into a ball. Dip the tops into the sugar mixture. Place sugar side up, 2 inches apart on greased baking sheets.

4. Bake for 8 minutes in the preheated oven. Let cool for 3 to 4 minutes on the baking sheets before removing to wire racks to cool completely.

Adam's Dirt Cookies

Submitted by: **Adam Mitchell**

Makes: 4 dozen

Preparation: 10 minutes

Cooking: 20 minutes

Total: 1 hour 30 minutes

"Why smash perfectly good cookies just to make another batch of cookies? 'Cause they're YUMMY! Made with crushed sandwich cookies, the small pieces of broken cookie dust make the dough speckled - I've been told they look like they're made with dirt!"

INGREDIENTS

2¼ cups all-purpose flour

1 teaspoon baking soda

1 teaspoon salt

1 cup white sugar

½ cup packed brown sugar

1 cup butter, softened

2 eggs

1 teaspoon vanilla extract

1½ cups chocolate sandwich cookie crumbs

DIRECTIONS

1. Sift together the flour, baking soda, and salt. Set aside. In a medium bowl, cream the white sugar, brown sugar, and the butter together until smooth. Stir in the eggs and vanilla. Add the flour mixture, and stir until just combined. Stir the crushed cookies into the dough. Cover, and chill the dough for ½ hour.

2. Preheat the oven to 375°F (190°C). Grease cookie sheets.

3. Drop dough by rounded spoonfuls onto prepared cookie sheets. Bake for 10 to 11 minutes in the preheated oven. Remove to cool on wire racks.

Chocolate Sandwich Cookies

Submitted by: **Lisa Lepsy**

Makes: 2 dozen

Preparation: 30 minutes

Cooking: 8 minutes

Total: 1 hour 10 minutes

"Excellent frozen. I have played with this over the years, and come up with several variations. At the holidays, I have added 1 teaspoon peppermint extract to the filling in lieu of the vanilla, and have also used crushed peppermint candy in the filling. I have also dipped them in chocolate, and coated them in confectioners' sugar."

INGREDIENTS

3 cups all-purpose flour

1½ cups white sugar

¾ cup unsweetened cocoa powder

¾ teaspoon salt

3 teaspoons baking powder

1½ cups milk

2 eggs

1½ teaspoons vanilla extract

¾ cup shortening

¾ cup butter, softened

2 cups confectioners' sugar

⅛ teaspoon salt

1 (7 ounce) jar marshmallow creme

1½ teaspoons vanilla extract

1 tablespoon milk

DIRECTIONS

1. Preheat oven to 400°F (200°C).

2. In a large bowl, combine flour, white sugar, cocoa powder, ¾ teaspoon salt, and baking powder. Stir in 1½ cups milk, eggs, 1½ teaspoons vanilla, and shortening. Mix until smooth using an electric mixer. Drop batter by rounded teaspoons onto ungreased cookie sheets. Leave space, and only use a teaspoon; these spread.

3. Bake in preheated oven for 7 to 8 minutes. Remove from pan immediately, and cool on wire rack.

4. To make the filling, combine the butter, confectioners' sugar, 1/8 teaspoon salt, marshmallow creme, 1 1/2 teaspoons vanilla, and 1 tablespoon milk in a medium bowl. Beat with mixer until fluffy. Spread filling on one cookie, and top with another sandwich style.

Best Big, Fat, Chewy Chocolate Chip Cookie

Makes: 1½ dozen

Preparation: 10 minutes

Cooking: 15 minutes

Total: 40 minutes

Submitted by: **Elizabeth**

"These cookies are the pinnacle of perfection! If you want a big, fat, chewy cookie like the kind you see at bakeries and specialty shops, then these are the cookies for you!"

INGREDIENTS

2 cups all-purpose flour

½ teaspoon baking soda

½ teaspoon salt

¾ cup unsalted butter, melted

1 cup packed brown sugar

½ cup white sugar

1 tablespoon vanilla extract

1 egg

1 egg yolk

2 cups semisweet chocolate chips

DIRECTIONS

1. Preheat the oven to 325°F (165°C). Grease cookie sheets or line with parchment paper.

2. Sift together the flour, baking soda and salt; set aside.

3. In a medium bowl, cream together the melted butter, brown sugar and white sugar until well blended. Beat in the vanilla, egg, and egg yolk until light and creamy. Mix in the sifted ingredients until just blended. Stir in the chocolate chips by hand using a wooden spoon. Drop cookie dough ¼ cup at a time onto the prepared cookie sheets. Cookies should be about 3 inches apart.

4. Bake for 15 to 17 minutes in the preheated oven, or until the edges are lightly toasted. Cool on baking sheets for a few minutes before transferring to wire racks to cool completely.

Ashley's Chocolate Chip Cookies

Submitted by: **Ashley Stay**

Makes: 3 dozen

Preparation: 10 minutes

Cooking: 8 minutes

Total: 35 minutes

"I was only 14 when I made up this recipe. Since my first batch, it's been everybody's favorite. If you follow the directions and measurements exactly, I promise that this will be your favorite chocolate chip cookie recipe."

INGREDIENTS

1²/₃ cups all-purpose flour

³/₄ teaspoon baking powder

¹/₂ teaspoon salt

³/₄ cup butter, softened

³/₄ cup packed brown sugar

¹/₃ cup white sugar

1 egg

1 teaspoon vanilla extract

2 cups milk chocolate chips

DIRECTIONS

1. Preheat the oven to 375°F (190°C).

2. Sift together the flour, baking powder, and salt; set aside.

3. In a medium bowl, cream together the butter, brown sugar, and white sugar until smooth. Beat in the egg and vanilla. Gradually stir in the sifted ingredients, then stir in the chocolate chips. Drop by rounded tablespoonfuls onto ungreased cookie sheets.

4. Bake for 8 to 10 minutes in preheated oven. Allow cookies to cool on baking sheet for 5 minutes before transferring to a wire rack to cool completely.

Light Chocolate Chip Cookies

Submitted by: **Megan Noble**

Makes: 24 cookies

Preparation: 15 minutes

Cooking: 10 minutes

Total: 35 minutes

"This is a tasty recipe for soft and chewy chocolate chip cookies. Don't try to double it though, it doesn't turn out."

INGREDIENTS

3/4 cup packed brown sugar

1/4 cup white sugar

6 tablespoons butter

1/2 teaspoon vanilla extract

1 egg white

3 tablespoons water

1 1/2 cups all-purpose flour

3/4 teaspoon baking soda

1/4 teaspoon salt

1/2 cup semisweet chocolate chips

DIRECTIONS

1. Preheat oven to 350°F (175°C).

2. In a medium bowl, cream the butter with the brown and white sugars. Stir in the vanilla, egg white, and water. Sift together the flour, baking soda, and salt; stir into the creamed mixture. Mix in the chocolate chips.

3. Drop dough by heaping spoonfuls onto ungreased cookie sheets. Bake for 8 to 10 minutes in the preheated oven. Allow cookies to cool for 1 minute on baking sheets before transferring to wire racks to cool completely.

Best Ever Chocolate Chip Cookies

Submitted by: **Jaylor**

Makes: 7 dozen

Preparation: 20 minutes

Cooking: 15 minutes

Total: 1 hour 35 minutes

"This recipe was such a hit when I was at college, my roommates still call and ask for it. You may add more chocolate chips if you really like chocolate!"

INGREDIENTS

3 cups margarine, softened

2½ cups white sugar

2½ cups packed brown sugar

2 teaspoons vanilla extract

4 eggs

8 cups all-purpose flour

4 teaspoons baking soda

1 teaspoon salt

4 cups semisweet chocolate chips

DIRECTIONS

1. Preheat oven to 350°F (175°C).

2. In a large bowl, cream together margarine, white sugar, and brown sugar until smooth. Beat in the eggs and vanilla. In a separate bowl, mix together flour, baking soda, and salt. Add to egg mixture, and mix well. Stir in chocolate chips. Instead of just dropping them onto the cookie sheet, I roll the cookies into balls - it makes them all look very uniform and nice!

3. Bake in preheated oven for 12 to 15 minutes, or until light brown. Cool on a wire rack.

Cake Mix Cookies VII

Submitted by: **Angela**

Makes: 2 dozen

Preparation: 5 minutes

Cooking: 10 minutes

Total: 40 minutes

"A twist on plain old cake or cookies. Great combos of the optional ingredients - toffee bits, walnuts, peanut butter chips - make this recipe everyone's personal favorite."

INGREDIENTS

1 (18.5 ounce) package yellow cake mix

1 teaspoon baking powder

2 eggs

½ cup vegetable oil

1 cup semisweet chocolate chips or other goodies

DIRECTIONS

1. Preheat oven to 350°F (175°C).

2. In a medium bowl, stir together the cake mix and baking powder. Add eggs and oil, then mix until well blended. Stir in chocolate chips, or your choice of additions. Drop by rounded spoonfuls onto cookie sheets.

3. Bake for 8 to 10 minutes in the preheated oven. Bake less for chewy cookies and more for crispy cookies. Allow cookies to cool on baking sheets for 5 minutes before transferring to a wire rack to cool completely.

Award Winning Soft Chocolate Chip Cookies

Submitted by: **Debbi Borsick**

Makes: 6 dozen

Preparation: 15 minutes

Cooking: 12 minutes

Total: 1 hour 40 minutes

"Everybody wants this recipe when I take them in for a carry-in. To make them award winning, my daughter, Tegan, made them for a cookie baking contest and won a red ribbon! You can use any flavor pudding you like for this recipe."

INGREDIENTS

4½ cups all-purpose flour

2 teaspoons baking soda

2 cups butter, softened

1½ cups packed brown sugar

½ cup white sugar

2 (3.4 ounce) packages instant vanilla pudding mix

4 eggs

2 teaspoons vanilla extract

4 cups semisweet chocolate chips

2 cups chopped walnuts (optional)

DIRECTIONS

1. Preheat oven to 350°F (175°C). Sift together the flour and baking soda, set aside.

2. In a large bowl, cream together the butter, brown sugar, and white sugar. Beat in the instant pudding mix until blended. Stir in the eggs and vanilla. Blend in the flour mixture. Finally, stir in the chocolate chips and nuts. Drop cookies by rounded spoonfuls onto ungreased cookie sheets.

3. Bake for 10 to 12 minutes in the preheated oven. Edges should be golden brown.

Best Chocolate Chip Cookies

Submitted by: **Dora**

Makes: 4 dozen

Preparation: 20 minutes

Cooking: 10 minutes

Total: 1 hour

"Crisp edges, chewy middles."

INGREDIENTS

1 cup butter, softened

1 cup white sugar

1 cup packed brown sugar

2 eggs

2 teaspoons vanilla extract

3 cups all-purpose flour

1 teaspoon baking soda

2 teaspoons hot water

½ teaspoon salt

2 cups semisweet chocolate chips

1 cup chopped walnuts

DIRECTIONS

1. Preheat oven to 350°F (175°C).

2. Cream together the butter, white sugar, and brown sugar until smooth. Beat in the eggs one at a time, then stir in the vanilla. Dissolve baking soda in hot water. Add to batter along with salt. Stir in flour, chocolate chips, and nuts. Drop by large spoonfuls onto ungreased pans.

3. Bake for about 10 minutes in the preheated oven, or until edges are nicely browned.

Best Chocolate Chippers

Submitted by: **Tina Holcombe**

Makes: 4 dozen

Preparation: 15 minutes

Cooking: 15 minutes

Total: 1 hour

"These are the BEST chocolate chip cookies I have ever made; and I have been testing different ingredients for a long time. I hope you love them as much as my guys do!!! I use a wooden spoon to mix these, as the texture seems to be so much better."

INGREDIENTS

1 cup butter

1 cup vegetable oil

1 cup white sugar

1 cup packed brown sugar

2 eggs

1 teaspoon vanilla extract

4$1/2$ cups all-purpose flour

2 teaspoons baking soda

4 teaspoons cream of tartar

1 teaspoon salt

2 cups semisweet chocolate chips

1 cup chopped walnuts (optional)

DIRECTIONS

1. Preheat the oven to 350°F (175°C).

2. In a large bowl, cream together the butter, oil, brown sugar, and white sugar until smooth. Beat in the eggs and vanilla. Combine the flour, baking soda, cream of tartar, and salt; stir into the creamed mixture. Mix in the chocolate chips and walnuts. Drop dough by rounded teaspoons onto ungreased cookie sheets.

3. Bake for 12 to 15 minutes in the preheated oven, or until light brown. Allow cookies to cool on the baking sheets for a couple of minutes before transferring to wire racks to cool completely.

Chocolate Chip Cookies for Special Diets

Submitted by: **Bernie**

Makes: 4 dozen

Preparation: 15 minutes

Cooking: 12 minutes

Total: 50 minutes

"Be sure to use a heat-stable sugar substitute. Since the substitutes vary in strength, use an amount equal to 3/4 cup regular sugar according to the package."

INGREDIENTS

½ cup butter, softened

¾ cup granulated artificial sweetener

2 tablespoons water

½ teaspoon vanilla extract

1 egg, beaten

1⅛ cups all-purpose flour

½ teaspoon baking soda

½ teaspoon salt

½ cup semisweet chocolate chips

½ cup chopped pecans

DIRECTIONS

1. Preheat oven to 375°F (190°C).

2. In a medium bowl, cream together the butter and sugar substitute. Mix in water, vanilla, and egg. Sift together the flour, baking soda, and salt; stir into the creamed mixture. Mix in the chocolate chips and pecans. Drop cookies by heaping teaspoonfuls onto a cookie sheet.

3. Bake in the preheated oven for 10 to 12 minutes. Remove from cookie sheets to cool on wire racks. These cookies freeze well.

Macadamia Nut Chocolate Chip Cookies

Submitted by: **Bev**

Makes: 3 dozen

Preparation: 15 minutes

Cooking: 12 minutes

Total: 40 minutes

"Drop cookies with macadamia nuts and chocolate chips!"

INGREDIENTS

1/2 cup butter, softened

1/3 cup packed dark brown sugar

1/3 cup white sugar

1 egg

1 teaspoon vanilla extract

1 1/8 cups sifted all-purpose flour

1/2 teaspoon baking soda

1/2 teaspoon salt

1 cup macadamia nuts, chopped

1 1/4 cups semisweet chocolate chips

DIRECTIONS

1. Preheat oven to 375°F (190°C). Lightly grease 2 large cookie sheets with vegetable shortening.

2. Cream the butter and sugars together in a large bowl. Beat in the egg and vanilla extract until well blended. Sift together the flour, baking soda, and salt; gradually blend into the batter. Stir in the chopped macadamia nuts and chocolate chips. Drop by rounded teaspoonfuls onto the cookie sheets, about 2 inches apart.

3. Bake in preheated oven for 10 to 12 minutes, or until the cookies are golden brown. Remove from the oven, and transfer the cookies to cooling racks.

Stephen's Chocolate Chip Cookies

Submitted by: Wendy Peppel

Makes: 4 dozen

Preparation: 15 minutes

Cooking: 12 minutes

Total: 50 minutes

"I created this recipe for my father on his birthday. It contains lots of different chocolates and nuts. Thanks Dad for sending me to cookie baking school at the San Francisco Culinary Academy! This one is just for you!"

INGREDIENTS

1 cup butter

1 cup brown sugar

1 cup white sugar

2 eggs

1 teaspoon vanilla extract

2½ cups all-purpose flour

1 teaspoon baking soda

1 teaspoon baking powder

½ teaspoon salt

⅔ cup white chocolate chips

⅔ cup milk chocolate chips

⅔ cup semisweet chocolate chips

⅓ cup chopped walnuts

⅓ cup chopped pecans

⅓ cup chopped almonds

DIRECTIONS

1. Preheat the oven to 350°F (175°C).

2. In a medium bowl, cream together the butter, brown sugar, and white sugar. Mix in the eggs and vanilla. Combine the flour, baking soda, baking powder, and salt; add to butter mixture, and stir until just blended. With a large wooden spoon, stir in the white, milk, and semi-sweet chocolate chips. Stir in the walnuts, pecans, and almonds. Drop dough by heaping spoonfuls onto ungreased cookie sheets.

3. Bake for 10 to 12 minutes in the preheated oven. Allow cookies to cool on the baking sheet before transferring to wire racks to cool completely.

Allison's Supreme Chocolate Chip Cookies

Submitted by: **Maria Allison**

Makes: 2 dozen

Preparation: 15 minutes

Cooking: 12 minutes

Total: 40 minutes

"Extra rich chocolate chip cookies. These stay soft a long time!"

INGREDIENTS

1/2 cup shortening

1/2 cup butter, softened

3/4 cup packed brown sugar

3/4 cup white sugar

2 eggs

1 teaspoon vanilla extract

1 tablespoon coffee-flavored liqueur

2 cups all-purpose flour

1 teaspoon baking soda

1 teaspoon salt

2 cups rolled oats

2 cups semisweet chocolate chips

1 cup chopped walnuts

DIRECTIONS

1. Preheat oven to 375°F (190°C). Grease cookie sheets.

2. In a large bowl, cream together the shortening, butter, brown sugar, and white sugar until smooth. Beat in the eggs one at a time, then stir in the vanilla and coffee liqueur. Combine the flour, baking soda, and salt; stir into the sugar mixture. Mix in the oats, chocolate chips, and walnuts. Roll tablespoonfuls of dough into balls, and place them 2 inches apart onto the prepared cookie sheets.

3. Bake for 10 to 12 minutes in the preheated oven, or until golden. Cool on a wire rack for a few minutes before eating!

Urban Legend Chocolate Chip Cookies

Submitted by: **Rene Kratz**

Makes: 5 dozen

Preparation: 15 minutes

Cooking: 8 minutes

Total: 1 hour

"You may have heard this story...a woman asks to buy a cookie recipe and is told it will cost 'two-fifty.' She thinks this means $2.50, but then she gets her credit card bill back and finds out it is $250.00. Outraged, she spreads the recipe far and wide to try and get her money's worth. I first heard this story six years ago and was given a recipe on a sheet of paper which bore the date '1986.' The supposed originator of the recipe was a well-known cookie company. I have since heard this tale again several times, with the recipe originating from different upscale department stores. True story? Who knows, but it's a darn good cookie. Here's my version."

INGREDIENTS

1 cup butter, softened

1 cup white sugar

1 cup packed brown sugar

2 eggs

1 teaspoon vanilla extract

2 cups all-purpose flour

2½ cups rolled oats

½ teaspoon salt

1 teaspoon baking powder

1 teaspoon baking soda

2 cups semisweet chocolate chips

4 ounces milk chocolate, grated

1½ cups chopped walnuts

DIRECTIONS

1. Preheat oven to 375°F (190°C). Measure oats into a blender or food processor, and then blend to a fine powder. Set aside.

2. In a large bowl, cream together butter and sugars. Beat in the eggs one at a time, then stir in the vanilla. In a separate bowl, mix together flour, oats, salt, baking powder, and baking soda. Stir dry ingredients into creamed butter and sugar. Add chocolate chips, grated chocolate, and nuts.

3. Drop by rounded teaspoons onto ungreased cookie sheets. Bake for 6 to 8 minutes in the preheated oven.

Chewy Chocolate Cookies

Submitted by: **Linda Whittaker**

Makes: 4 dozen

Preparation: 15 minutes

Cooking: 10 minutes

Total: 55 minutes

"These are GREAT chocolate chocolate chip cookies. Always a request at Christmas from friends and family!"

INGREDIENTS

1¼ cups butter, softened

2 cups white sugar

2 eggs

2 teaspoons vanilla extract

2 cups all-purpose flour

¾ cup unsweetened cocoa powder

1 teaspoon baking soda

½ teaspoon salt

2 cups semisweet chocolate chips

DIRECTIONS

1. Preheat oven to 350°F (175°C).

2. In a large bowl, cream together the butter and sugar until light and fluffy. Beat in the eggs one at a time, then stir in the vanilla. Sift together the flour, cocoa, baking soda, and salt; stir into the creamed mixture. Mix in the chocolate chips. Drop dough by teaspoonfuls onto ungreased cookie sheets.

3. Bake 8 to 9 minutes in the preheated oven. Cookies will be soft. Cool slightly on cookie sheet; remove from sheet onto wire rack to cool completely.

Chocolate Chocolate Chip Cookies

Submitted by: **Kathy Brandt**

Makes: 4 dozen

Preparation: 15 minutes

Cooking: 10 minutes

Total: 45 minutes

"These cookies are great...you get a double dose of chocolate! My kids love them."

INGREDIENTS

1 cup butter, softened

1½ cups white sugar

2 eggs

2 teaspoons vanilla extract

2 cups all-purpose flour

⅔ cup cocoa powder

¾ teaspoon baking soda

¼ teaspoon salt

2 cups semisweet chocolate chips

½ cup chopped walnuts (optional)

DIRECTIONS

1. Preheat oven to 350°F (175°C).

2. In large bowl, beat butter, sugar, eggs, and vanilla until light and fluffy. Combine the flour, cocoa, baking soda, and salt; stir into the butter mixture until well blended. Mix in the chocolate chips and walnuts. Drop by rounded teaspoonfuls onto ungreased cookie sheets.

3. Bake for 8 to 10 minutes in the preheated oven, or just until set. Cool slightly on the cookie sheets before transferring to wire racks to cool completely.

Mocha Chocolate Cookies

Submitted by: **Robin**

Makes: 4 dozen

Preparation: 25 minutes

Cooking: 12 minutes

Total: 40 minutes

"I call these 'Moaners.' A rich dark cookie."

INGREDIENTS

2 cups semisweet chocolate chips, divided

2 tablespoons boiling water

2 tablespoons instant coffee powder

1/2 cup butter, softened

1/2 cup white sugar

1/2 cup packed brown sugar

1 egg

1 1/4 cups all-purpose flour

3/4 teaspoon baking soda

1/2 teaspoon salt

1 cup chopped walnuts

DIRECTIONS

1. Preheat oven to 350°F (175°C). Melt 1/2 cup chocolate chips in microwave or double-boiler, stirring occasionally until smooth. Cool to room temperature. In a small bowl, dissolve instant coffee in boiling water; set aside.

2. In a large bowl, cream together the butter, white sugar, and brown sugar until smooth. Beat in egg, coffee, and melted chocolate. Combine flour, baking soda, and salt; mix into batter. Stir in the remaining chocolate chips and walnuts. Drop dough by heaping teaspoons onto ungreased cookie sheets.

3. Bake for 10 to 12 minutes in preheated oven. Allow to stand 2 to 3 minutes on the cookie sheets before transferring to wire racks to cool completely.

Absolutely Sinful Chocolate Chocolate Chip Cookies

Submitted by: **Marsha**

Makes: 2 dozen

Preparation: 15 minutes

Cooking: 12 minutes

Total: 40 minutes

"This recipe was given to me by my grandmother 10 years ago. They were always a HUGE hit at work pig-outs and now my family loves them! A wonderful soft cookie that is incredibly chocolaty."

INGREDIENTS

2 1/2 (1 ounce) squares unsweetened chocolate

1/2 cup butter

2 cups all-purpose flour

1/2 teaspoon baking soda

1 teaspoon baking powder

1/4 teaspoon salt

1 1/4 cups white sugar

2 eggs

1 teaspoon vanilla extract

2/3 cup sour cream

2 cups semisweet chocolate chips

DIRECTIONS

1. Preheat oven to 375 °F (190°C). In the microwave or over a double boiler, melt unsweetened chocolate and butter together, stirring occasionally until smooth. Sift together flour, baking soda, baking powder, and salt; set aside.

2. In a medium bowl, beat sugar, eggs, and vanilla until light. Mix in the chocolate mixture until well blended. Stir in the sifted ingredients alternately with sour cream, then mix in chocolate chips. Drop by rounded tablespoonfuls onto ungreased cookie sheets.

3. Bake for 8 to 10 minutes in the preheated oven. Allow cookies to cool on baking sheet for 5 minutes before transferring to a wire rack to cool completely. Store in an airtight container.

Mechelle's Chocolate Cookies

Submitted by: **Mechelle**

Makes: 6 dozen

Preparation: 15 minutes

Cooking: 12 minutes

Total: 1 hour

"Nutty and super chocolaty cookies that use three kinds of chocolate chips. If you love chocolate as much as I do, you will love these cookies. Hope they last more than a day!!"

INGREDIENTS

1 cup blanched slivered almonds, toasted

4 (1 ounce) squares bittersweet chocolate, chopped

1½ cups semisweet chocolate chips

4 (1 ounce) squares milk chocolate, chopped

2 cups rolled oats

2 cups all-purpose flour

1 teaspoon baking powder

1 teaspoon baking soda

½ teaspoon salt

1 cup butter, softened

1 cup packed brown sugar

1 cup white sugar

2 eggs

2 teaspoons vanilla extract

DIRECTIONS

1. Preheat oven to 350°F (175°C). Grease or butter cookie sheets.

2. In a small bowl, toss together almonds, bittersweet, semisweet and milk chocolate pieces, and oats; set aside. Sift together flour, baking powder, baking soda, and salt; set aside.

3. In a large bowl, cream together butter, brown sugar, and white sugar until smooth. Beat in eggs one at a time, then stir in the vanilla. Stir in the flour mixture until just blended; Mix in oats, nuts, and chocolates. Drop dough by tablespoonfuls onto the prepared cookie sheets.

4. Bake for 12 to 15 minutes in the preheated oven. Allow cookies to cool on baking sheets for 2 minutes before transferring to a wire racks to cool completely.

Chocolate Chip Meringue Drops

Submitted by: **S.N. Noble**

Makes: 40 cookies

Preparation: 15 minutes

Cooking: 3 hours

Total: 3 hours 15 minutes

"These are lower in fat than most cookies and do not last long, so be prepared to make them often!"

INGREDIENTS

2 egg whites

1/2 cup white sugar

1 teaspoon vanilla extract

3 tablespoons unsweetened cocoa powder

1/2 cup semisweet chocolate chips

DIRECTIONS

1. Preheat oven to 250°F (120°C). Line 2 baking sheets with aluminum foil or parchment paper, and set aside.

2. In large metal or glass bowl, beat the egg whites on high speed with an electric mixer until soft peaks form. Gradually add sugar while continuing to beat until they hold stiff peaks. Mix in the vanilla and cocoa on low speed, then fold in chocolate chips by hand. Drop small mounds of the mixture onto the prepared baking sheets, spacing 1 inch apart.

3. Bake for 1 hour in the preheated oven. Turn off oven, and leave the cookies in the oven for 2 more hours, or until centers are dry. Remove from pan and store in an airtight container.

Chocolate Chip Shortbread Cookie Logs

Submitted by: **Rhonda Golub**

Makes: 4 dozen

Preparation: 30 minutes

Cooking: 10 minutes

Total: 1 hour

"Delicious shortbread logs with chocolate chips in the cookie and dipped in chocolate and nuts on the end."

INGREDIENTS

1 cup butter, softened

½ cup sifted confectioners' sugar

1 teaspoon vanilla extract

2 cups all-purpose flour

2 cups mini semisweet chocolate chips, divided

1 tablespoon shortening

¾ cup finely chopped walnuts

DIRECTIONS

1. Preheat oven to 350°F (175°C). Grease cookie sheets.

2. Cream together butter and confectioners' sugar until smooth. Stir in vanilla. Mix in the flour, and then one cup of the chocolate chips. Shape dough into 2x½ inch logs. Place logs 2 inches apart on prepared cookie sheets.

3. Bake for 10 to 13 minutes in preheated oven, or until firm. Let cookies cool completely before removing from pan (shortbread is brittle).

4. Melt the remaining 1 cup chocolate chips and shortening over a double boiler, stirring frequently until smooth. Dip one end of each cookie into the chocolate, then into the nuts. Place onto waxed paper until set.

White Chocolate Chunk Cookies

Submitted by: **Donna**

Makes: 2 dozen

Preparation: 15 minutes

Cooking: 15 minutes

Total: 3 hours 15 minutes

"A delicious cookie with chunks of white chocolate and macadamia nuts. A great combination."

INGREDIENTS

½ cup butter, softened

½ cup shortening

¾ cup white sugar

½ cup packed brown sugar

1 egg

1¾ cups all-purpose flour

1 teaspoon baking soda

½ teaspoon salt

2 teaspoons vanilla extract

10 ounces white chocolate, chopped

½ cup chopped and toasted macadamia nuts

DIRECTIONS

1. In a large bowl, cream butter and shortening; gradually add sugars, beating well at medium speed with an electric mixer. Beat in egg and vanilla. Combine flour, soda, and salt; stir into creamed mixture. Stir in white chocolate and macadamia nuts. Chill dough for 1 hour.

2. Preheat oven to 350°F (175°C). Lightly grease cookie sheets. Drop dough by heaping tablespoonfuls 3 inches apart onto prepared cookie sheets.

3. Bake for 12 to 14 minutes in preheated oven. Cookies will be soft. Cool slightly on cookie sheets; transfer to wire racks to cool completely.

White Chocolate Macadamia Nut Cookies III

Submitted by: **Mary**

Makes: 4 dozen

Preparation: 15 minutes

Cooking: 10 minutes

Total: 45 minutes

"I was served this cookie at a restaurant in Springfield, MO during a business conference. Went home and made up this recipe which has been a hit at any church gathering when I take them...better than the one I had at the conference."

INGREDIENTS

1 cup butter, softened

3/4 cup packed light brown sugar

1/2 cup white sugar

2 eggs

1/2 teaspoon vanilla extract

1/2 teaspoon almond extract

2 1/2 cups all-purpose flour

1 teaspoon baking soda

1/2 teaspoon salt

1 cup coarsely chopped macadamia nuts

1 cup coarsely chopped white chocolate

DIRECTIONS

1. Preheat oven to 350°F (175°C).

2. In a large bowl, cream together the butter, brown sugar, and white sugar until smooth. Beat in the eggs, one at a time, then stir in the vanilla and almond extracts. Combine the flour, baking soda, and salt; gradually stir into the creamed mixture. Mix in the macadamia nuts and white chocolate. Drop dough by teaspoonfuls onto ungreased cookie sheets.

3. Bake for 10 minutes in the preheated oven, or until golden brown.

Orange Cream Cookies

Submitted by: **Mary**

Makes: 4 dozen

Preparation: 20 minutes

Cooking: 12 minutes

Total: 1 hour 15 minutes

"Cookies that taste like the ultimate childhood treat...orange cream ice cream."

INGREDIENTS

3/4 cup shortening

1 1/2 cups packed brown sugar

2 eggs

1 teaspoon vanilla extract

3 cups all-purpose flour

3 tablespoons orange flavored drink mix (e.g. Tang®)

1 1/2 teaspoons baking powder

1/2 teaspoon salt

1 teaspoon baking soda

1/2 cup buttermilk

1 cup white chocolate chips

1 teaspoon butter

3 tablespoons orange flavored drink mix (e.g. Tang®)

1 cup confectioners' sugar

3 tablespoons water

DIRECTIONS

1. Preheat oven to 375°F (190°C). Lightly grease baking sheets.

2. Cream the shortening and brown sugar together until light. Beat in the eggs and vanilla. Combine the flour, 3 tablespoons drink mix, baking powder, and salt. Dissolve the baking soda into the buttermilk. Stir in the flour mixture alternately with the buttermilk mixture. Stir in the white chocolate chips. Drop dough by teaspoonfuls onto prepared cookie sheets.

3. Bake for 10 to 12 minutes. Frost cookies while still hot with orange glaze.

4. In a small bowl, blend together the butter, 3 tablespoons orange drink mix, and confectioners sugar until smooth. Mix in water 2 teaspoons at a time until a pourable consistency is reached. Drizzle or brush onto cookies while still warm.

White Chocolate Orange Cookies

Submitted by: **Jennifer**

Makes: 3 dozen cookies

Preparation: 15 minutes

Cooking: 12 minutes

Total: 50 minutes

"These are my new personal favorites!"

INGREDIENTS

1 cup butter, softened

1/2 cup white sugar

1/2 cup packed brown sugar

1 egg

1 tablespoon orange zest

2 1/4 cups all-purpose flour

3/4 teaspoon baking soda

1/2 teaspoon salt

2 cups white chocolate chips

1 cup chopped walnuts

DIRECTIONS

1. Preheat oven to 350°F (175°C).

2. Cream the butter and sugars together until light and fluffy. Beat in the egg and orange zest. Stir the flour, baking soda, and salt together; mix into the creamed mixture. Stir in the white chocolate chips and chopped walnuts. Drop tablespoonfuls of dough onto ungreased baking sheets.

3. Bake for 10 to 12 minutes in the preheated oven. Allow to cool on the baking sheet for 2 minutes before transferring to a wire rack to cool completely.

White Chocolate and Cranberry Cookies

Submitted by: **Diane Abed**

Makes: 2 dozen

Preparation: 15 minutes

Cooking: 10 minutes

Total: 50 minutes

"I make a basic chocolate chip cookie dough, but use white chocolate chips, dried cranberries, and brandy (instead of vanilla). Great for Christmas time!"

INGREDIENTS

½ cup butter, softened

½ cup packed brown sugar

½ cup white sugar

1 egg

1 tablespoon brandy

1½ cups all-purpose flour

½ teaspoon baking soda

¾ cup white chocolate chips

1 cup dried cranberries

DIRECTIONS

1. Preheat oven to 375 °F (190°C). Grease cookie sheets.

2. In a large bowl, cream together the butter, brown sugar, and white sugar until smooth. Beat in the egg and brandy. Combine the flour and baking soda; stir into the sugar mixture. Mix in the white chocolate chips and cranberries. Drop by heaping spoonfuls onto prepared cookie sheets.

3. Bake for 8 to 10 minutes in the preheated oven. For best results, take them out while they are still doughy. Allow cookies to cool for 1 minute on the cookie sheets before transferring to wire racks to cool completely.

Banana Chocolate Chip Cookies

Submitted by: **Evelyn Brown**

Makes: 3 dozen

Preparation: 15 minutes

Cooking: 15 minutes

Total: 1 hour 15 minutes

"This recipe uses very ripe bananas, the ones which you would not want to eat. The riper the bananas are, the more flavor they have."

INGREDIENTS

2¹/₂ cups all-purpose flour

2 teaspoons baking powder

¹/₂ teaspoon salt

¹/₄ teaspoon baking soda

1 cup white sugar

²/₃ cup butter, softened

2 eggs

1 teaspoon vanilla extract

1 cup mashed bananas

2 cups semisweet chocolate chips

DIRECTIONS

1. Preheat oven to 400°F (200°C). Grease cookie sheets. Sift the flour, baking powder, salt, and baking soda together, and set aside.

2. Cream the butter with the sugar until light and fluffy. Beat in the eggs and vanilla. Mix in the mashed bananas. Add the flour mixture, and stir until just combined. Stir in the chocolate chips. Drop by spoonfuls onto prepared cookie sheets.

3. Bake in preheated oven for 12 to 15 minutes.

A to Z Everything-but-the-Kitchen-Sink Chocolate Chip Cookies

Makes: 5 dozen

Preparation: 30 minutes

Cooking: 10 minutes

Total: 1 hour 10 minutes

Submitted by: **Melissa**

"This the most amazing cookie recipe that I have ever baked! It has oats, chocolate chips, coconut, cornflakes, walnuts, plus much more - They're chewy, crispy, crunchy and fabulous! No one could get enough! I just had to share this with you all! Enjoy!"

INGREDIENTS

1¹/₂ cups all-purpose flour	1 cup white sugar
1¹/₄ teaspoons baking soda	2 eggs
1 teaspoon salt	1 tablespoon milk
1¹/₂ teaspoons ground cinnamon	1¹/₂ teaspoons vanilla extract
¹/₂ teaspoon ground mace	1 cup cornflakes cereal, crumbled
¹/₈ teaspoon ground nutmeg	3 cups rolled oats
¹/₈ teaspoon ground cloves	¹/₂ cup flaked coconut
1 cup butter, softened	2 cups semisweet chocolate chips
1¹/₂ cups packed brown sugar	1 cup chopped walnuts

DIRECTIONS

1. Preheat oven to 350°F (175°C). Grease cookie sheets. Sift together flour, baking soda, salt, cinnamon, mace, nutmeg, and cloves; set aside.

2. In a large bowl, cream together butter, brown sugar, and white sugar until smooth. Beat in the eggs one at a time, then stir in milk and vanilla. Gradually mix in the sifted ingredients until well blended. Using a wooden spoon, stir in the cornflakes, oats, coconut, chocolate chips, and walnuts. Roll the dough into walnut sized balls, and place 2 inches apart on prepared cookie sheets; flatten slightly.

3. Bake for 8 to 10 minutes in preheated oven. Allow cookies to cool on baking sheet for 5 minutes before transferring to a wire rack to cool completely. I found that slightly under baking these yields wonderfully chewy cookies!

sugar cookies

Sugar cookies represent the cookie in its purest form. Based on three simple ingredients — flour, sugar, and butter — these cookies are delicate but subtly flavorful. They also present the perfect cookie-canvas for creativity: texture them with nuts, flavor them with citrus, decorate them with icing — unleash your inner artist!

Dawn's Sugar Cookies

Submitted by: **Dawn**

Makes: 2 dozen

Preparation: 35 minutes

Cooking: 10 minutes

Total: 1 hour 15 minutes

"I received this buttermilk-sugar cookie recipe from a friend in Shipshewana, IN which has a large Amish community. A beautiful place to visit!!!"

INGREDIENTS

1 cup shortening

2 cups white sugar

4 eggs

1 teaspoon vanilla extract

4 cups all-purpose flour

2 teaspoons baking powder

1 teaspoon baking soda

1 cup buttermilk

½ cup butter, melted

2 cups confectioners' sugar

2 tablespoons milk

3 drops red food coloring (optional)

DIRECTIONS

1. Preheat oven to 350°F (175°C). Line cookie sheets with parchment paper.

2. In a large bowl, cream together the shortening and white sugar until smooth. Beat in eggs one at a time, and stir in vanilla. Combine the flour, baking powder, and baking soda; stir into the creamed mixture alternately with the buttermilk until a soft dough forms. Drop by teaspoonfuls onto prepared cookie sheets.

3. Bake for 10 minutes in preheated oven, or until light brown. Cool on wire racks.

4. In a medium bowl, blend together melted butter and confectioners' sugar until smooth. Gradually stir in milk until frosting reaches the desired consistency. Mix in food coloring, if desired. Spread onto cooled cookies, and place frosted cookies on waxed paper or cooling racks until frosting is set.

Amish Cookies

Submitted by: **Alice Hoff**

Makes: 5 dozen

Preparation: 10 minutes

Cooking: 10 minutes

Total: 1 hour

"This recipe is used by the Amish in the Midwest...around Wisconsin and Iowa."

INGREDIENTS

1 cup butter, softened

1 cup vegetable oil

1 cup white sugar

1 cup confectioners' sugar

2 eggs

1/2 teaspoon vanilla extract

4 1/2 cups all-purpose flour

1 teaspoon baking soda

3/4 teaspoon cream of tartar

DIRECTIONS

1. Preheat the oven to 375°F (190°C). Grease cookie sheets.

2. In a large bowl, mix together the butter, oil, white sugar, and confectioners' sugar until smooth. Beat in the eggs one at a time, then stir in the vanilla. Combine the flour, baking soda, and cream of tartar. Stir into the sugar mixture until just combined. Drop dough by teaspoonfuls onto the prepared cookie sheets.

3. Bake for 8 to 10 minutes in preheated oven, or until bottoms are lightly browned. Remove from baking sheets to cool on wire racks.

Mississippi Tea Cakes

Submitted by: **Carol K.**

"This is my mother's recipe, her mother's recipe, and so on... Basic, simple, down-home and delicious!! My grandmother's advice is to enjoy warm with a big glass of ice-cold milk!!! Poor folks' heaven!!!"

INGREDIENTS

½ cup butter, softened

1 cup white sugar

1 egg

1 teaspoon vanilla extract

2 cups all-purpose flour

1 teaspoon baking powder

½ teaspoon baking soda

¼ cup buttermilk

DIRECTIONS

1. Preheat oven to 350°F (175°C). Grease cookie sheets.

2. In a medium bowl, cream together butter and sugar until smooth. Beat in egg and vanilla. Combine flour, baking powder, and baking soda; beat into the creamed mixture alternately with the buttermilk. Drop by rounded spoonfuls onto prepared cookie sheets.

3. Bake for 8 to 10 minutes in preheated oven. Allow cookies to cool on baking sheets for 5 minutes before transferring to a wire rack to cool completely.

Angel Crisps

Submitted by: **Paula**

Makes: 4 dozen

Preparation: 20 minutes

Cooking: 20 minutes

Total: 40 minutes

"It's a great recipe if you like sugar cookies. Easy to make and they go fast in my house."

INGREDIENTS

½ cup butter

½ cup shortening

½ cup brown sugar, packed

½ cup white sugar

1 egg

1 teaspoon vanilla extract

2 cups all-purpose flour

1 teaspoon cream of tartar

1 teaspoon baking soda

½ teaspoon salt

½ cup white sugar for decoration

DIRECTIONS

1. Preheat the oven to 425°F (220°C).

2. In a large bowl, cream together butter, shortening, brown sugar, and ½ cup white sugar until smooth. Beat in the egg, and stir in the vanilla. Combine the flour, cream of tartar, baking soda, and salt; beat into the creamed mixture.

3. Roll dough into 1 inch balls. Dip the top half of the balls into water, then into remaining white sugar. Place sugar side up onto ungreased cookie sheets. Flatten slightly.

4. Bake for 8 to 10 minutes in preheated oven, or until light brown. Cool on wire racks, and store in an airtight container.

Cream Cheese Cookies

Submitted by: **Robin**

Makes: 6 dozen

Preparation: 10 minutes

Cooking: 15 minutes

Total: 1 hour

"These cookies are delicate when made with a press, or hardy when dropped by spoonfuls. I fill centers of press cookies with preserves or a chocolate chip for added variety."

INGREDIENTS

1 cup butter, softened

1 (3 ounce) package cream cheese, softened

1 cup white sugar

1 egg yolk

1/2 teaspoon vanilla extract

2 1/2 cups all-purpose flour

DIRECTIONS

1. Preheat oven to 325°F (165°C). Lightly grease cookie sheets.

2. In a large bowl, cream together butter, cream cheese, and sugar until light and fluffy. Beat in egg yolk and vanilla. Stir in flour until well blended. Drop dough by spoonfuls or use a cookie press to place onto prepared cookie sheets. If using floral cookie press design, make an indentation in the center with a thimble, fill with preserves, or press candy into center.

3. Bake for 15 minutes in preheated oven. Cookies should be pale.

Cream Cheese Cookies IV

Submitted by: **Madonna**

Makes: 3 dozen

Preparation: 15 minutes

Cooking: 10 minutes

Total: 1 hour 15 minutes

"This is a quick and easy cream cheese cookie."

INGREDIENTS

¼ cup butter, softened

1 (8 ounce) package cream cheese

1 egg yolk

¼ teaspoon vanilla extract

1 (18.5 ounce) package yellow cake mix

DIRECTIONS

1. In a large bowl, cream together the butter and cream cheese. Blend in the egg yolk and vanilla. Gradually beat in the cake mix. Dough will be stiff. Cover, and chill for 30 minutes.

2. Preheat oven to 375°F (190°C). Grease cookie sheets. Drop dough by rounded teaspoonfuls onto the prepared cookie sheets.

3. Bake for 8 to 10 minutes in the preheated oven, or until firm. Cool on wire racks.

Sugar Cookie Drops

Submitted by: **Lois**

Makes: 6 dozen

Preparation: 15 minutes

Cooking: 10 minutes

Total: 1 hour 25 minutes

"A crisp cookie that melts in your mouth."

INGREDIENTS

1 cup butter

1 cup vegetable oil

1½ cups confectioners' sugar

1 cup white sugar

2 eggs

1 teaspoon vanilla extract

4½ cups all-purpose flour

1 teaspoon baking soda

1 teaspoon cream of tartar

½ cup white sugar for decoration

DIRECTIONS

1. Preheat oven 350°F (175°C).

2. In a large bowl, cream together the butter, oil, confectioners' sugar, and 1 cup white sugar until light and fluffy. Beat in eggs one at a time, and stir in the vanilla. Combine the flour, baking soda, and cream of tartar; stir into the creamed mixture. Roll dough into 1 inch balls, and then roll the balls in remaining white sugar. Place onto ungreased cookie sheets, and flatten with a fork.

3. Bake for 8 to 10 minutes in the preheated oven, or until the edges begin to brown. Cool on wire racks.

Melt - In - Your - Mouth Shortbread

Submitted by: **Jennifer Wilton**

Makes: 2 dozen

Preparation: 10 minutes

Cooking: 15 minutes

Total: 25 minutes

"This quick and easy shortbread will literally melt when you take a bite. Great for Christmas parties with a little bit of decorating."

INGREDIENTS

1 cup butter, softened

1/2 cup confectioners' sugar

1/4 cup cornstarch

1 1/2 cups all-purpose flour

DIRECTIONS

1. Preheat the oven to 375°F (190°C).

2. Whip butter with an electric mixer until fluffy. Stir in the confectioners' sugar, cornstarch, and flour. Beat on low for one minute, then on high for 3 to 4 minutes. Drop cookies by spoonfuls 2 inches apart on an ungreased cookie sheet.

3. Bake for 12 to 15 minutes in the preheated oven. Watch that the edges don't brown too much. Cool on wire racks.

Ricotta Cookies II

Submitted by: **Sandy**

Makes: 8 dozen

Preparation: 25 minutes

Cooking: 10 minutes

Total: 1 hour 50 minutes

"Delicate Italian ricotta cookies with an almond flavored glaze. Very good!"

INGREDIENTS

½ pound butter

1¾ cups white sugar

2 eggs

15 ounces ricotta cheese

2 tablespoons vanilla extract

4 cups all-purpose flour

1 teaspoon baking powder

1 teaspoon baking soda

5 tablespoons milk

1½ cups confectioners' sugar

1 teaspoon almond extract

¼ cup colored candy sprinkles

DIRECTIONS

1. Preheat oven to 350°F (175°C).

2. In a medium bowl, cream together butter, sugar, eggs, ricotta cheese, and vanilla extract. Combine the flour, baking powder, and baking soda; blend into the creamed mixture, mixing in additional flour as necessary to form a workable dough. Roll dough into teaspoon-sized balls, and arrange on an ungreased cookie sheet.

3. Bake 8 to 10 minutes in the preheated oven, until lightly browned.

4. In a medium bowl, beat milk, confectioners' sugar, and almond extract until smooth. Spoon over warm cookies, and sprinkle with colored candy sprinkles.

Black and White Cookies

Submitted by: **Mary Jane**

Makes: 2 dozen

Preparation: 20 minutes

Cooking: 30 minutes

Total: 1 hour 20 minutes

"New York black and white deli cookies."

INGREDIENTS

1 cup unsalted butter

1³/4 cups white sugar

4 eggs

1 cup milk

1/2 teaspoon vanilla extract

1/4 teaspoon lemon extract

2¹/2 cups cake flour

2¹/2 cups all-purpose flour

1 teaspoon baking powder

1/2 teaspoon salt

4 cups confectioners' sugar

1/3 cup boiling water

1 (1 ounce) square bittersweet chocolate, chopped

DIRECTIONS

1. Preheat oven to 375°F (190°C). Butter 2 baking sheets.

2. In a medium bowl, cream together butter and sugar until smooth. Beat in eggs one at a time, then stir in the milk, vanilla, and lemon extract. Combine cake flour and all-purpose flour, baking powder, and salt; gradually blend into the creamed mixture. Drop tablespoonfuls of the dough 2 inches apart on prepared baking sheets.

3. Bake until edges begin to brown, about 20 to 30 minutes. Cool completely.

4. Place confectioners sugar in large bowl. Mix in boiling water one tablespoon at a time until mixture is thick and spreadable. (Add more than the indicated amount if you need to).

5. Transfer half of the frosting to the top of a double boiler set over simmering water. Stir in the chocolate. Warm mixture, stirring frequently, until the chocolate melts. Remove from heat.

6. With a brush, coat half the cookie with chocolate frosting and the other half with the white frosting. Set on waxed paper until frosting hardens.

Nutty Crispy Sugar Cookies

Submitted by: **Cindy Carnes**

Makes: 5 dozen

Preparation: 20 minutes

Cooking: 12 minutes

Total: 1 hour 10 minutes

"I worked with a woman that baked 80 dozen or more cookies during the holidays. Every day she brought 1/2 dozen of every cookie she'd baked the night before; this is my favorite. I sometimes roll the dough into balls and then roll them in some granulated sugar rather than making these as drop cookies. These freeze well."

INGREDIENTS

5 cups all-purpose flour

2 teaspoons baking soda

2 teaspoons cream of tartar

¼ teaspoon salt

1 cup butter

2 cups white sugar

2 eggs

1 cup vegetable oil

1 teaspoon vanilla extract

¾ cup chopped walnuts

DIRECTIONS

1. Preheat oven to 350°F (175°C). Lightly grease cookie sheets. Stir together the flour, baking soda, cream of tartar, and salt; set aside.

2. In a large bowl, cream together the butter and sugar until smooth. Beat in eggs, vegetable oil, and vanilla. Gradually stir in flour mixture until smooth. Stir in nuts. Drop dough by rounded teaspoonfuls onto the prepared cookie sheets. Flatten cookies with a fork.

3. Bake in the preheated oven for 10 to 12 minutes, or until the edges begin to brown. Cool on baking sheets for a minute before transferring to wire racks to cool completely.

Brown Butter Cookies

Submitted by: **Heather**

Makes: 5 dozen

Preparation: 30 minutes

Cooking: 10 minutes

Total: 1 hour 20 minutes

"Using butter (NOT margarine) is essential for the success of this rich, but highly addictive cookie! You may need as little as 3 cups confectioners' sugar for the icing; just stop adding it when you've reached the desired consistency."

INGREDIENTS

2 cups butter

2 cups brown sugar

2 eggs

2 teaspoons vanilla extract

1 teaspoon baking soda

1/2 teaspoon baking powder

1/2 teaspoon salt

3 cups all-purpose flour

2/3 cup chopped pecans

2 teaspoons vanilla extract

3 1/2 cups confectioners' sugar

1/2 cup hot water

DIRECTIONS

1. Preheat oven to 350°F (175°C).

2. Heat butter over medium heat for 5 minutes or so, until it turns nut brown in color. The foaming and bubbling is part of the browning process, but watch it carefully so that you don't burn the butter. Remove from heat, and cool slightly. Reserve 1/2 cup of the butter f or the frosting.

3. Pour remaining browned butter into a large mixing bowl. Beat browned butter with brown sugar until the butter is no longer hot. Mix in eggs, 2 teaspoons vanilla, baking soda, baking powder, and salt. Beat thoroughly. Mix in flour and chopped pecans. Drop tablespoons of dough onto ungreased baking sheets.

4. Bake for 10 minutes in the preheated oven, or until light brown around the edges. Cool.

5. In a medium bowl, mix the reserved 1/2 cup browned butter with 2 teaspoons vanilla, confectioners' sugar, and hot water. Beat until smooth, and use to frost cooled cookies.

Chewy Coconut Cookies

Submitted by: **N. Hoff**

Makes: 3 dozen

Preparation: 30 minutes

Cooking: 10 minutes

Total: 50 minutes

"Lots of coconut and sugar make these cookies chewy and delicious."

INGREDIENTS

1¼ cups all-purpose flour

½ teaspoon baking soda

¼ teaspoon salt

½ cup butter

½ cup packed brown sugar

½ cup white sugar

1 egg

½ teaspoon vanilla extract

1⅓ cups flaked coconut

DIRECTIONS

1. Preheat oven to 350°F (175°C.) Combine the flour, baking soda, and salt; set aside.

2. In a medium bowl, cream the butter, brown sugar, and white sugar until smooth. Beat in the egg and vanilla until light and fluffy. Gradually blend in the flour mixture, then mix in the coconut. Drop dough by teaspoonfuls onto an ungreased cookie sheet. Cookies should be about 3 inches apart.

3. Bake for 8 to 10 minutes in the preheated oven, or until lightly toasted. Cool on wire racks.

Potato Chip Cookies II

Submitted by: **Barbara**

Makes: 2 dozen

Preparation: 20 minutes

Cooking: 14 minutes

Total: 48 minutes

"This recipe adds pecans for extra flavor."

INGREDIENTS

1 cup butter

½ cup white sugar

1 egg yolk

1 teaspoon vanilla extract

1½ cups all-purpose flour

⅔ cup crushed potato chips

1 cup chopped pecans

DIRECTIONS

1. Preheat oven to 350°F (175°C).

2. In a medium bowl, cream together butter and sugar until smooth. Stir in egg yolk and vanilla. Gradually stir in the flour until just blended, then mix in crushed potato chips and pecans. Drop by rounded spoonfuls onto ungreased cookie sheets. Criss-cross the top using a fork dipped in water.

3. Bake 12 to 14 minutes in preheated oven, or until edges are lightly browned. Cool on baking sheets.

Lemon Sugar Tea Cookies

Submitted by: **Tamme**

Makes: 4 dozen

Preparation: 25 minutes

Cooking: 12 minutes

Total: 2 hours

"Delightful lemon flavored cookies."

INGREDIENTS

3/4 cup butter

2 cups white sugar

1 egg

2 tablespoons corn syrup

1 teaspoon lemon extract

2 cups all-purpose flour

1 teaspoon baking soda

1 teaspoon baking powder

DIRECTIONS

1. In a medium bowl, cream together butter and 1 cup sugar until light and fluffy. Beat in egg, corn syrup, and lemon extract. Stir in flour, baking soda, and baking powder. Cover dough, and chill in the refrigerator at least 1 hour.

2. Preheat oven to 325°F (165°C). Line a cookie sheet with parchment paper. Roll chilled dough into walnut sized balls. Roll balls in remaining sugar, and place on the prepared cookie sheet.

3. Bake 12 minutes in the preheated oven, or until lightly browned.

Lemon Meltaways

Submitted by: **Susan Lewis**

Makes: 4 dozen

Preparation: 20 minutes

Cooking: 12 minutes

Total: 3 hours 20 minutes

"These frosted lemon cookies are a delicious refrigerator cookie, and they are quick and easy to make."

INGREDIENTS

¾ cup butter, softened

⅓ cup confectioners' sugar

1 tablespoon lemon juice

1 teaspoon lemon zest

1¼ cups all-purpose flour

½ cup corn starch

¾ cup confectioners' sugar

¼ cup butter, softened

1 teaspoon lemon juice

1 teaspoon lemon zest

DIRECTIONS

1. In a medium bowl, cream together ¾ cup butter and ⅓ cup confectioners' sugar until smooth. Stir in 1 tablespoon lemon juice and 1 teaspoon lemon zest. Combine the flour and corn starch, and blend into the lemon mixture to form a soft dough. Divide dough in half, roll each half into a log about 8 inches long and 1 inch in diameter. Wrap in plastic wrap and refrigerate for 2 hours, or until firm.

2. Preheat oven to 350°F (175°C). Cut each roll into ¼ inch slices and place onto the cookie sheet.

3. Bake in the preheated oven for 8 to 12 minutes, or until set. Cool completely before frosting.

4. In a small bowl, blend together ¾ cup confectioners' sugar, ¼ cup butter, 1 teaspoon lemon juice, and 1 teaspoon lemon zest with an electric mixer until smooth. Frost cookies and allow to dry before serving or storing.

Lemonade Cookies

Submitted by: **Kathleen Dickerson**

Makes: 3 dozen

Preparation: 15 minutes

Cooking: 20 minutes

Total: 40 minutes

"Lemonade concentrate makes these simple cookies a tart treat!"

INGREDIENTS

1 cup butter

1 cup white sugar

2 eggs

3 cups sifted all-purpose flour

1 teaspoon baking soda

1 (6 ounce) can lemonade concentrate, thawed

2 tablespoons white sugar

DIRECTIONS

1. Preheat oven to 400°F (200°C). Lightly grease a cookie sheet.

2. In a large bowl, cream together butter and 1 cup sugar. Blend in eggs. In a medium bowl, sift together flour and baking soda; gradually beat into butter mixture, alternating with ½ cup lemonade concentrate. Drop mixture by rounded teaspoons onto the prepared cookie sheet.

3. Bake 8 to 10 minutes in the preheated oven, until lightly brown. Brush lightly with remaining lemonade, and sprinkle with remaining sugar.

Spring Lime Tea Cookies

Submitted by: **Christina Pierson**

Makes: 2 dozen

Preparation: 20 minutes

Cooking: 10 minutes

Total: 50 minutes

"These are light, buttery tea cookies bursting with citrus flavor. Perfect for a spring day."

INGREDIENTS

2 teaspoons lime juice

1/3 cup milk

1/2 cup butter, softened

3/4 cup white sugar

1 egg

2 teaspoons lime zest

1 3/4 cups all-purpose flour

1 teaspoon baking powder

1/4 teaspoon baking soda

2 tablespoons lime juice

1/4 cup white sugar

DIRECTIONS

1. Preheat oven to 350°F (175°C). Combine the 2 teaspoons of lime juice with the milk, let stand for 5 minutes.

2. In a large bowl, cream together the butter and 3/4 cup sugar until light and fluffy. Beat in the egg, then stir in the lime zest and milk mixture. Combine the flour, baking powder and baking soda, blend into the creamed mixture. Drop by rounded spoonfuls onto the ungreased cookie sheets.

3. Bake for 8 to 10 minutes in the preheated oven, until the edges are light brown. Allow cookies to cool on baking sheets for 5 minutes before transferring to a wire rack to cool completely.

4. To make the glaze, stir together the remaining lime juice and sugar. Brush onto cooled cookies.

Key Lime Cookies

Submitted by: **Pam**

Makes: 3 dozen

Preparation: 20 minutes

Cooking: 10 minutes

Total: 50 minutes

"Lime flavored rolled cookies."

INGREDIENTS

½ cup butter

1 cup white sugar

1 egg

1 egg yolk

1½ cups all-purpose flour

1 teaspoon baking powder

½ teaspoon salt

¼ cup fresh lime juice

1½ teaspoons grated lime zest

½ cup confectioners' sugar for decoration

DIRECTIONS

1. Preheat oven to 350°F (175°C). Grease cookie sheets.

2. In a large bowl, cream butter, sugar, egg, and egg yolk until smooth. Stir in lime juice and lime zest. Combine the flour, baking powder, and salt; blend into the creamed mixture. Form dough into ½ inch balls, and arrange on the prepared cookie sheet.

3. Bake 8 to 10 minutes in the preheated oven, or until lightly browned. Cool on wire racks. Sift confectioners' sugar over cookies while still warm.

Banana Bread Cookies

Submitted by: **Molly**

Makes: 3 dozen

Preparation: 20 minutes

Cooking: 15 minutes

Total: 1 hour

"These are soft, chewy cookies that taste just like homemade banana bread!"

INGREDIENTS

1 cup butter flavored shortening

1 cup white sugar

2 eggs

1 teaspoon vanilla extract

1 banana, peeled and mashed

2 cups all-purpose flour

1 teaspoon baking soda

1/2 teaspoon salt

3 tablespoons butter

1/3 cup confectioners' sugar

1 tablespoon milk

1 teaspoon vanilla extract

DIRECTIONS

1. Preheat oven to 350°F (175°C). Lightly grease baking sheets.

2. In a medium bowl, cream together shortening and white sugar until smooth. Beat in eggs, vanilla extract, and banana. Combine flour, baking soda, and salt; blend thoroughly into the shortening mixture to make a sticky batter. Drop by rounded tablespoons onto the prepared baking sheets.

3. Bake 10 to 15 minutes in the preheated oven, or until lightly browned.

4. In a medium bowl, blend butter, confectioners' sugar, milk and vanilla extract. Adjust amount of milk as necessary to attain a drizzling consistency. Drizzle over warm cookies.

Banana Pudding Sugar Cookies

Submitted by: **Tina Grinnell**

Makes: 2½ dozen

Preparation: 15 minutes

Cooking: 10 minutes

Total: 2 hours 35 minutes

"Guaranteed to stay moist as long as you don't leave them out."

INGREDIENTS

⅔ cup shortening

⅔ cup white sugar

2 eggs

1 teaspoon vanilla extract

½ teaspoon baking powder

½ teaspoon salt

1 (3.5 ounce) package instant banana pudding mix

2½ cups all-purpose flour

DIRECTIONS

1. In a medium bowl, cream together shortening and sugar until light and fluffy. Beat in eggs one at a time. Stir in vanilla extract, baking powder, salt, and instant banana pudding mix. Mix in 2 cups flour. Gradually mix in remaining ½ cup flour as needed to form a workable dough. Cover, and chill in the refrigerator at least 2 hours.

2. Preheat oven to 375°F (190°C). Grease baking sheets. Shape dough into walnut sized balls, and place 2 inches apart on the prepared baking sheets. Flatten balls to a thickness of about ¼ inch.

3. Bake 8 to 10 minutes in the preheated oven, or until lightly browned.

Banana Split Cookies

Submitted by: **Carol Gutt**

Makes: 2 1/2 dozen

Preparation: 15 minutes

Cooking: 10 minutes

Total: 1 hour 35 minutes

"I received this recipe from my retired school-teaching Aunt who selected this as her all-time favorite cookie recipe from the many years of teaching and having students bring in their favorite cookies."

INGREDIENTS

1/2 cup butter

1 cup packed brown sugar

2 eggs

1 cup mashed bananas

2 cups all-purpose flour

2 teaspoons baking powder

1/4 teaspoon baking soda

1/4 teaspoon salt

1/2 teaspoon ground cinnamon

1/4 teaspoon ground cloves

1/2 cup chopped walnuts

DIRECTIONS

1. In a medium bowl, cream together the butter and brown sugar. Beat in the eggs and mashed banana. Sift together the flour, baking powder, baking soda, salt, cinnamon, and cloves; blend into the banana mixture. Stir in the nuts. Cover, and chill for at least 1 hour.

2. Preheat the oven to 375°F (190°C). Lightly grease cookie sheets. Drop dough by rounded teaspoons onto the prepared cookie sheets.

3. Bake for 8 to 10 minutes in the preheated oven, or until no imprint remains when touched. Cool on wire racks.

Great Grandad's Sugar Cookies

Submitted by: **Kathylee**

Makes: 5 dozen

Preparation: 30 minutes

Cooking: 10 minutes

Total: 1 hour 10 minutes

"This recipe puffs up to make great Sugar cookies. My Great Grandfather was a baker, and this is the kind the bakery made. To make sour milk, add a teaspoon of vinegar to regular milk, and let stand for 5 minutes."

INGREDIENTS

6 cups all-purpose flour

1 tablespoon baking powder

1 teaspoon ground nutmeg

1 pinch salt

2½ cups white sugar

1½ cups shortening

1 teaspoon baking soda

1 cup sour milk

3 eggs, beaten

1 teaspoon vanilla extract

DIRECTIONS

1. Preheat oven to 350°F (175°C). Line cookie sheets with parchment paper.

2. In a medium bowl, stir together 4 cups flour, baking powder, nutmeg, salt, and sugar. Cut in the shortening until the mixture resembles coarse crumbs. Stir in baking soda, sour milk, beaten eggs, and vanilla. Stir as little as possible, and add the remaining flour as necessary to make dough thick enough to roll out.

3. On a lightly floured surface, roll out dough ¼ inch thick. Cut into desired shapes with cookie cutters. Place cookies 1 inch apart on the prepared cookie sheets.

4. Bake for 8 to 10 minutes in preheated oven. Cool on baking sheets.

Soft Christmas Cookies

Submitted by: **Georgie Bowers**

Makes: 4 dozen

Preparation: 20 minutes

Cooking: 8 minutes

Total: 3 hours

"Soft cut out sugar cookie that I have used for years. I sprinkle with colored sugar before baking or you could also try icing them when cool."

INGREDIENTS

3¾ cups all-purpose flour

1 teaspoon baking powder

½ teaspoon salt

1 cup margarine, softened

1½ cups white sugar

2 eggs

2 teaspoons vanilla extract

DIRECTIONS

1. Sift flour, baking powder, and salt together, set aside. In a large bowl, cream together the margarine and sugar until light and fluffy. Beat in the eggs one at a time, then stir in the vanilla. Gradually blend in the sifted ingredients until fully absorbed. Cover dough, and chill for 2 hours.

2. Preheat oven to 400°F (200°C). Grease cookie sheets. On a clean floured surface, roll out small portions of chilled dough to ¼ inch thickness. Cut out shapes using cookie cutters.

3. Bake 6 to 8 minutes in the preheated oven, or until edges are barely brown. Remove from cookie sheets to cool on wire racks.

The Best Rolled Sugar Cookies

Submitted by: **Jill Saunders**

Makes: 5 dozen

Preparation: 45 minutes

Cooking: 8 minutes

Total: 3 hours

"Whenever you make these cookies for someone, be sure to bring along several copies of the recipe! You will be asked for it, I promise!!! NOTE: I make icing with confectioners' sugar and milk. I make it fairly thin, as I 'paint' the icing on the cookies with a pastry brush. Thin enough to spread easily but not so thin that it just makes your cookies wet and runs off."

INGREDIENTS

1½ cups butter, softened

2 cups white sugar

4 eggs

1 teaspoon vanilla extract

5 cups all-purpose flour

2 teaspoons baking powder

1 teaspoon salt

DIRECTIONS

1. In a large bowl, cream together butter and sugar until smooth. Beat in eggs and vanilla. Stir in the flour, baking powder, and salt. Cover, and chill dough for at least one hour (or overnight).

2. Preheat oven to 400°F (200°C). Roll out dough on floured surface ¼ to ½ inch thick. Cut into shapes with any cookie cutter. Place cookies 1 inch apart on ungreased cookie sheets.

3. Bake 6 to 8 minutes in preheated oven. Cool completely.

Betz's Good Sugar Cookies

Submitted by: **Tricia Weimer**

Makes: 4 dozen

Preparation: 20 minutes

Cooking: 10 minutes

Total: 9 hours

"This recipe has been handed down from my great-great grandmother at least. We're not sure how far it goes back, but does go back to the early 1900's at least."

INGREDIENTS

1 cup butter

1½ cups white sugar

2 eggs

1 teaspoon vanilla extract

1 teaspoon lemon extract

2 cups all-purpose flour

1 teaspoon baking powder

1 pinch salt

DIRECTIONS

1. In a large bowl, cream together the butter and sugar until fluffy. Beat in the eggs one at a time, then stir in the vanilla and lemon extracts. Combine the flour, baking powder, and salt; gradually blend into the creamed mixture to form a soft dough. Cover or wrap dough, and refrigerate overnight.

2. Preheat the oven to 400°F (200°C). On a floured surface, roll the dough out ¼ inch thick. Cut into desired shapes using cookie cutters. Place cookies 2 inches apart on ungreased cookie sheets.

3. Bake for 10 minutes in the preheated oven, or until lightly browned. Cool on wire racks.

Vel's Christmas Shortbread

Submitted by: **Judy Smith**

Makes: 5 dozen

Preparation: 30 minutes

Cooking: 12 minutes

Total: 1 hour

"There are a lot of shortbread recipes out there, but these are special. Vel is my mom, and these are the best! At first it will seem that this dough will not go together, but after a lot of kneading, the butter will hold this dough together. You will get the greatest English shortbread that you have ever made."

INGREDIENTS

2 cups butter

1 cup brown sugar

5 cups sifted all-purpose flour

DIRECTIONS

1. Preheat oven to 350°F (175°C).

2. In a large bowl, cream butter and brown sugar until smooth. Sir in flour, and knead by hand until dough comes together. At first the dough will seem dry and crumbly but don't give up, keep mixing. Roll out the dough to ¼ inch thickness, and cut with cookie cutters or press dough into shortbread molds. Place cookies 2 inches apart onto ungreased cookie sheets.

3. Bake for 8 to 12 minutes in the preheated oven, depending on the size of your cookies. Do not let them brown. Remove from cookie sheets to cool on wire racks.

Easy Cut-Out Cookies

Submitted by: **Tina Curtis**

Makes: 3 dozen

Preparation: 5 minutes

Cooking: 10 minutes

Total: 2 hours 45 minutes

"This is the easiest and the best tasting sugar cookies you will eat. It's so easy kids will always request it!"

INGREDIENTS

2¼ cups all-purpose flour

1 cup confectioners' sugar

1 cup butter, melted

1 egg

1 teaspoon vanilla extract

DIRECTIONS

1. In a medium bowl, combine the flour and confectioners' sugar. Stir in the melted butter, egg, and vanilla until well blended. Cover, and refrigerate dough for at least 2 hours.

2. Preheat oven to 350°F (175°C). Line baking sheets with parchment paper.

3. On a lightly floured surface, roll the dough out ¼ inch thick. Cut into desired shapes using cookie cutters.

4. Bake for 8 to 10 minutes in the preheated oven. Allow cookies to cool on baking sheet for 5 minutes before transferring to a wire rack to cool completely.

Cream Cheese Sugar Cookies

Submitted by: **Karin Christian**

Makes: 6 dozen

Preparation: 15 minutes

Cooking: 10 minutes

Total: 9 hours 25 minutes

"A soft, chewy, and flavorful sugar cookie. It is very important to chill the dough, as it is too sticky to roll unless well chilled."

INGREDIENTS

1 cup white sugar

1 cup butter, softened

1 (3 ounce) package cream cheese, softened

1/2 teaspoon salt

1/2 teaspoon almond extract

1/2 teaspoon vanilla extract

1 egg yolk

2 1/4 cups all-purpose flour

DIRECTIONS

1. In a large bowl, combine the sugar, butter, cream cheese, salt, almond and vanilla extracts, and egg yolk. Beat until smooth. Stir in flour until well blended. Chill the dough for 8 hours, or overnight.

2. Preheat oven to 375°F (190°C).

3. On a lightly floured surface, roll out the dough 1/3 at a time to 1/8 inch thickness, refrigerating remaining dough until ready to use. Cut into desired shapes with lightly floured cookie cutters. Place 1 inch apart on ungreased cookie sheets. Leave cookies plain for frosting, or brush with slightly beaten egg white and sprinkle with candy sprinkles or colored sugar.

4. Bake for 7 to 10 minutes in the preheated oven, or until light and golden brown. Cool cookies completely before frosting.

Butter Icing for Cookies

Submitted by: **Barbara**

Makes: 2½ cups

Preparation: 10 minutes

Total: 10 minutes

"Perfect for cookies - not too soft - not too hard - just right."

INGREDIENTS

2 cups confectioners' sugar

2½ tablespoons cream

4 tablespoons butter

1 teaspoon vanilla extract

DIRECTIONS

1. In a saucepan, over medium heat, heat cream and butter until butter is melted. Stir in the vanilla and confectioners' sugar. Remove from heat, and beat with an electric mixer until thick and smooth.

Sugar Cookie Frosting

Submitted by: **Kathy Brandt**

Makes: 3 cups

Preparation: 15 minutes

Total: 15 minutes

"Add food coloring to decorate your favorite sugar cookies."

INGREDIENTS

4 cups confectioners' sugar

½ cup shortening

5 tablespoons milk

1 teaspoon vanilla extract

food coloring (optional)

DIRECTIONS

1. In a large bowl, cream together the confectioners' sugar and shortening until smooth. Gradually mix in the milk and vanilla with an electric mixer until smooth and stiff, about 5 minutes. Color with food coloring if desired.

Buttercream Icing

Submitted by: **Sharon Gerstman**

Makes: 2 -1/2 cups

Preparation: 15 minutes

Total: 15 minutes

"An easy to make egg-free frosting that works great for decorating cookies for holidays, birthdays and parties. When you need to add coloring to icing, use color paste. If you use liquid coloring, you may need to add more confectioner's sugar."

INGREDIENTS

1/2 cup shortening

1/2 cup butter, softened

1 teaspoon vanilla extract

4 cups confectioners' sugar

2 tablespoons milk

DIRECTIONS

1. In a large bowl, cream together the butter, shortening, and vanilla. Blend in the sugar, one cup at a time, beating well after each addition. Beat in the milk, and continue mixing until light and fluffy. Keep icing covered until ready to decorate.

Decorator Frosting

Submitted by: **P. Oakes**

Makes: 2 cups

Preparation: 10 minutes

Total: 10 minutes

"A frosting that's perfect for sugar cookies."

INGREDIENTS

2/3 cup butter, softened

4 cups confectioners' sugar

2 tablespoons milk

1 teaspoon vanilla extract (optional)

4 drops red food coloring

DIRECTIONS

1. In a medium bowl, cream together the butter, confectioners' sugar, and milk until light and fluffy, about 3 to 4 minutes. Beat in the vanilla and food coloring. Spread on or between cookies.

Sugar Cookie Icing

Submitted by: **Janice Brubaker**

Makes: 1 dozen cookies' worth

Preparation: 15 minutes

Total: 15 minutes

"This icing dries hard and shiny and the colors stay bright. Choose as many different food colorings as you desire."

INGREDIENTS

1 cup confectioners' sugar

2 teaspoons milk

2 teaspoons light corn syrup

¼ teaspoon almond extract

assorted food coloring

DIRECTIONS

1. In a small bowl, stir together confectioners' sugar and milk until smooth. Beat in corn syrup and almond extract until icing is smooth and glossy. If icing is too thick, add more corn syrup.

2. Divide into separate bowls, and add food colorings to each to desired intensity. Dip cookies, or paint them with a brush.

Cream Cheese Frosting II

Submitted by: **Janni**

Makes: 3 cups

Preparation: 10 minutes

Total: 10 minutes

"This is a wonderfully creamy frosting that goes well with pumpkin bread, carrot cake, chocolate cake, on cookies, or between cookies. If you want chocolate frosting, add 1/4 to 1/2 cup cocoa, according to how rich you want it."

INGREDIENTS

2 (8 ounce) packages cream cheese, softened

½ cup butter, softened

2 cups sifted confectioners' sugar

1 teaspoon vanilla extract

DIRECTIONS

1. In a medium bowl, cream together the cream cheese and butter until creamy. Mix in the vanilla, then gradually stir in the confectioners' sugar. Store in the refrigerator after use.

oatmeal &
peanut butter

Crispy or chewy, spicy or nutty, with dried fruit, cereal, chocolate, or your favorite candy, these recipes carry fond memories of Grandma's house, home-town bakeries, and rainy-day after-school snacks. Oatmeal produces a hearty, rich cookie loaded with quick energy; peanut butter adds a creamy richness that melts in the mouth. These are the workhorses of the cookie kingdom and grace kids' lunch boxes everywhere.

Excellent Oatmeal Cookies

Submitted by: **Beatrice**

Makes: 3¹/₂ dozen

Preparation: 20 minutes

Cooking: 12 minutes

Total: 56 minutes

"This is a chewy oatmeal cookie."

INGREDIENTS

1 cup butter, softened

1 cup packed brown sugar

¹/₂ cup white sugar

2 eggs

2 teaspoons vanilla extract

1¹/₄ cups all-purpose flour

¹/₂ teaspoon baking soda

2 teaspoons ground cinnamon

1 teaspoon salt

3 cups quick cooking oats

1 cup chopped walnuts

DIRECTIONS

1. Preheat the oven to 325°F (165°C).

2. In a large bowl, cream together butter, brown sugar, and white sugar until fluffy. Beat in eggs one at a time, then stir in the vanilla. Combine the flour, baking soda, salt, and cinnamon; stir into the creamed mixture. Mix in oats and nuts until just blended. Drop by heaping teaspoonfuls onto ungreased cookie sheets. Cookies should be at least 2 inches apart.

3. Bake for about 12 minutes in the preheated oven. Cool cookies on a wire rack.

Cake Mix Cookies V

Submitted by: **Karen**

Makes: 3 dozen

Preparation: 15 minutes

Cooking: 10 minutes

Total: 45 minutes

"These cookies are easy to make, and so delicious. Oatmeal and walnuts add to the chewy texture."

INGREDIENTS

½ cup butter

2 eggs

1 (18.5 ounce) package yellow cake mix

⅔ cup quick cooking oats

½ cup finely chopped walnuts

DIRECTIONS

1. Preheat the oven to 375°F (190°C). Line baking sheets with parchment paper.

2. In a large bowl, mix butter and eggs until light and fluffy. Stir in cake mix, quick oats, and walnuts. Roll dough into walnut sized balls. Place cookies onto the prepared baking sheet, and flatten slightly with the bottom of a glass that has been buttered and dipped in sugar.

3. Bake for 8 to 10 minutes in preheated oven, or until golden brown. Allow cookies to cool on baking sheet for 5 minutes before transferring to a wire rack to cool completely.

Oatmeal Pudding Cookies

Submitted by: **Dawn**

Makes: 5 dozen

Preparation: 15 minutes

Cooking: 12 minutes

Total: 50 minutes

"Soft and chewy oatmeal cookies. The secret is in the pudding. These cookies are a favorite of my children."

INGREDIENTS

1 cup butter flavored shortening

3/4 cup packed brown sugar

1/4 cup white sugar

1 (3.5 ounce) package instant vanilla pudding mix

2 eggs

1 1/4 cups all-purpose flour

1 teaspoon baking soda

3 1/2 cups rolled oats

1 cup raisins (optional)

DIRECTIONS

1. Preheat oven to 350°F (175°C). Line baking sheets with parchment paper.

2. In a large bowl, cream together shortening, brown sugar, and white sugar until smooth. Blend in instant pudding, then beat in eggs until the batter is light and fluffy. Combine flour and baking soda; mix into the batter. Stir in oats and raisins. Dough will be stiff. Drop dough by spoonfuls onto the prepared baking sheets.

3. Bake for 8 to 12 minutes in the preheated oven, or until firm. Cool on wire racks.

Soft Oatmeal Cookies

Submitted by: **Barbara**

Makes: 2 dozen

Preparation: 15 minutes

Cooking: 10 minutes

Total: 2 hours

"These oatmeal cookies are very moist with a good flavor. Add a cup of raisins or nuts if you desire."

INGREDIENTS

1 cup butter, softened

1 cup white sugar

1 cup packed brown sugar

2 eggs

1 teaspoon vanilla extract

2 cups all-purpose flour

1 teaspoon baking soda

1 teaspoon salt

1½ teaspoons ground cinnamon

3 cups quick cooking oats

DIRECTIONS

1. In a medium bowl, cream together butter, white sugar, and brown sugar. Beat in eggs one at a time, then stir in vanilla. Combine flour, baking soda, salt, and cinnamon; stir into the creamed mixture. Mix in oats. Cover, and chill dough for at least one hour.

2. Preheat the oven to 375°F (190°C). Grease cookie sheets. Roll the dough into walnut sized balls, and place 2 inches apart on cookie sheets. Flatten each cookie with a large fork dipped in sugar.

3. Bake for 8 to 10 minutes in preheated oven. Allow cookies to cool on baking sheet for 5 minutes before transferring to a wire rack to cool completely.

Lacy Oatmeal Cookies

Submitted by: **Pookie**

Makes: 4 dozen

Preparation: 15 minutes

Cooking: 10 minutes

Total: 55 minutes

"This dough spreads to make thin, lacy, oatmeal cookies that you peel off the cookie sheet. Great served with ice cream, or rolled into tubes while still warm and dipped in chocolate."

INGREDIENTS

1 cup quick cooking oats

1/4 cup all-purpose flour

1/2 teaspoon salt

1 1/2 teaspoons baking powder

1 cup white sugar

1/2 cup butter, softened

1 egg

1 teaspoon vanilla extract

DIRECTIONS

1. Preheat oven to 325°F (165°C). Cover baking sheets with foil, then coat the foil with a non-stick cooking spray.

2. In a medium bowl, combine oats, flour, salt, and baking powder. In a large bowl, cream sugar and butter until fluffy. Beat in egg and vanilla. Mix in the flour and oat mixture until just combined. Drop dough by teaspoonfuls onto the prepared baking sheets, 2 1/2 inches apart.

3. Bake at 325°F (165°C) for 10 to 12 minutes, or until edges turn golden. Cool, then peel cookies off with your fingers. Be sure to re-spray baking sheets with non-stick cooking spray between batches.

Beth's Spicy Oatmeal Raisin Cookies

Submitted by: **Beth Sigworth**

Makes: 3 dozen

Preparation: 15 minutes

Cooking: 12 minutes

Total: 50 minutes

"With a little experimenting, I came up with these chewy, spicy, oatmeal raisin cookies. They make your kitchen smell wonderful while they are baking. They almost remind me of Christmas because the spices smell so good."

INGREDIENTS

½ cup butter, softened

½ cup butter flavored shortening

1 cup packed light brown sugar

½ cup white sugar

2 eggs

1 teaspoon vanilla extract

1½ cups all-purpose flour

1 teaspoon baking soda

1 teaspoon ground cinnamon

½ teaspoon ground cloves

½ teaspoon salt

3 cups rolled oats

1 cup raisins

DIRECTIONS

1. Preheat oven to 350°F (175°C).

2. In a large bowl, cream together the butter, butter flavored shortening, brown sugar, white sugar, eggs, and vanilla until smooth. Combine the flour, baking soda, cinnamon, cloves, and salt; stir into the sugar mixture. Stir in the oats and raisins. Drop by rounded teaspoonfuls onto ungreased cookie sheets.

3. Bake 10 to 12 minutes until light and golden. Do not overbake. Let them cool for 2 minutes before removing from cookie sheets to cool completely. Store in airtight container. Make sure you get some, because they don't last long!

Oatmeal Raisin Cookies

Submitted by: **Darlene**

"An old stand-by that the whole family loves."

INGREDIENTS

3/4 cup butter, softened

3/4 cup white sugar

3/4 cup packed light brown sugar

2 eggs

1 teaspoon vanilla extract

1¼ cups all-purpose flour

1 teaspoon baking soda

3/4 teaspoon ground cinnamon

1/2 teaspoon salt

2¾ cups rolled oats

1 cup raisins

DIRECTIONS

1. Preheat oven to 375°F (190°C).

2. In large bowl, cream together butter, white sugar, and brown sugar until smooth. Beat in the eggs and vanilla until fluffy. Stir together flour, baking soda, cinnamon, and salt. Gradually beat into butter mixture. Stir in oats and raisins. Drop by teaspoonfuls onto ungreased cookie sheets.

3. Bake 8 to 10 minutes in the preheated oven, or until golden brown. Cool slightly, remove from sheet to wire rack. Cool completely.

Bobbie's Oatmeal Cookies

Submitted by: **Shannon Wood**

Makes: 3 dozen
Preparation: 20 minutes
Cooking: 10 minutes
Total: 1 hour 5 minutes

"If you like oatmeal cookies, you will love these!! My husband says they are the best cookies I have ever made."

INGREDIENTS

1 cup butter, softened

1 cup packed brown sugar

1 cup white sugar

2 eggs

1 teaspoon vanilla extract

2 cups all-purpose flour

1 teaspoon baking soda

1/2 teaspoon salt

3 cups rolled oats

1/2 cup semisweet chocolate chips

1 cup raisins

1/2 cup chopped pecans

DIRECTIONS

1. Preheat oven to 350°F (175°C). Grease cookie sheets.

2. In a large bowl, cream together butter, brown sugar and white sugar until smooth. Beat in eggs and vanilla. Combine flour, baking soda, and salt; stir into the creamed mixture. Mix in the oats, chocolate chips, raisins, and pecans, one ingredient at a time. Drop by rounded spoonfuls onto the prepared cookie sheets.

3. Bake for 8 to 10 minutes in the preheated oven. Allow cookies to cool on baking sheet for 5 minutes before transferring to a wire rack to cool completely.

Grandmother's Oatmeal Cookies

Submitted by: **Sheryl Bohn**

Makes: 4 dozen

Preparation: 20 minutes

Cooking: 12 minutes

Total: 2 hours

"This is the best Oatmeal Cookie I have ever tasted and is my family's favorite. This is a recipe that I have had for years that a friend of mine gave me."

INGREDIENTS

3 eggs

1 cup raisins

1 teaspoon vanilla extract

1 cup butter flavored shortening

1 cup packed brown sugar

1 cup white sugar

2½ cups all-purpose flour

2 teaspoons baking soda

1 teaspoon salt

1 teaspoon ground cinnamon

2 cups quick cooking oats

½ cup chopped walnuts

DIRECTIONS

1. Beat eggs, and stir in raisins and vanilla. Refrigerate for at least an hour.

2. Preheat oven to 350°F (175°C).

3. Cream together shortening, brown sugar, and white sugar until light and fluffy. Combine flour, baking soda, salt, and cinnamon; stir into the sugar mixture. Mix in raisins and eggs, then stir in oats and walnuts. Roll dough into walnut sized balls, and place 2 inches apart on ungreased cookie sheets.

4. Bake for 10 to 12 minutes in preheated oven, or until edges are golden. Cool on wire racks.

Banana Oatmeal Cookies II

Submitted by: **Lois**

Makes: 3 dozen

Preparation: 10 minutes

Cooking: 15 minutes

Total: 1 hour 15 minutes

"This recipe is as close as I can get to the delicious cookies my mother use to make when I was a little girl. Spicy oatmeal cookies with banana and walnuts."

INGREDIENTS

3/4 cup shortening

1 cup packed brown sugar

1 egg

1/2 cup mashed ripe banana

1 teaspoon vanilla extract

1 cup all-purpose flour

1/2 teaspoon baking soda

1 teaspoon salt

1 teaspoon ground cinnamon

1/4 teaspoon ground cloves

3 cups rolled oats

1/2 cup chopped walnuts

DIRECTIONS

1. Preheat oven to 350°F (175°C). Grease cookie sheets.

2. In a large bowl, cream together shortening and brown sugar. Beat in egg and mashed banana, then stir in vanilla. Combine flour, baking soda, salt, cinnamon, and cloves; stir into the banana mixture. Mix in rolled oats and walnuts. Drop by rounded spoonfuls onto prepared cookie sheets. Leave room for spreading.

3. Bake for 8 to 10 minutes in preheated oven. Allow cookies to cool on cookie sheets for 5 minutes before transferring to a wire rack to cool completely.

Healthy Banana Cookies

Submitted by: **K.Gailbrath**

Makes: 3 dozen

Preparation: 15 minutes

Cooking: 20 minutes

Total: 1 hour 10 minutes

"These cookies are nutritious, as well as delicious."

INGREDIENTS

3 ripe bananas

2 cups rolled oats

1 cup dates, pitted and chopped

⅓ cup vegetable oil

1 teaspoon vanilla extract

DIRECTIONS

1. Preheat oven to 350°F (175°C).

2. In a large bowl, mash the bananas. Stir in oats, dates, oil, and vanilla. Mix well, and allow to sit for 15 minutes. Drop by teaspoonfuls onto an ungreased cookie sheet.

3. Bake for 20 minutes in the preheated oven, or until lightly brown.

Coffee Liqueur Raisin Cookies

Submitted by: **Missy**

Makes: 7 dozen

Preparation: 10 minutes

Cooking: 10 minutes

Total: 1 hour 30 minutes

"This is a wonderful, chewy, just a little different oatmeal cookie. I have made them with many variations and all of them good. They taste the best if the raisins soak in the coffee liqueur overnight."

INGREDIENTS

1 1/2 cups raisins

1/2 cup coffee flavored liqueur

1 cup shortening

2 cups packed brown sugar

3 eggs

1/2 cup milk

3 cups all-purpose flour

1 teaspoon baking powder

1 teaspoon baking soda

1/2 teaspoon salt

2 1/2 cups rolled oats

1 cup chopped walnuts (optional)

1 cup white chocolate chips (optional)

DIRECTIONS

1. Place raisins in a small bowl, and add coffee flavored liqueur. Heat in the microwave for approximately 2 minutes, or until hot. Set aside to cool (overnight is great). Drain, and reserve liquid.

2. Preheat oven to 350°F (175°C). Grease cookie sheets.

3. In a large bowl, cream together shortening and brown sugar. Beat in eggs, one at a time, then mix in milk and the reserved liquid from the raisins. Combine flour, baking powder, baking soda, and salt; stir into the creamed mixture. Stir in oats. Mix in the walnuts and white chocolate chips, if desired. Drop by rounded spoonfuls onto prepared cookie sheets.

4. Bake for 8 to 10 minutes in the preheated oven. Allow cookies to cool on baking sheet for 5 minutes before transferring to a wire rack to cool completely.

Oatmeal Cranberry White Chocolate Chunk Cookies

Makes: 2¹/₂ dozen

Preparation: 20 minutes

Cooking: 12 minutes

Total: 44 minutes

Submitted by: **Christina**

"Oatmeal cookies using dried cranberries and white chocolate chips, or you can use chocolate chips if you wish."

INGREDIENTS

²/₃ cup butter, softened

²/₃ cup packed brown sugar

2 eggs

1¹/₂ cups rolled oats

1¹/₂ cups all-purpose flour

¹/₂ teaspoon salt

1 teaspoon baking soda

1¹/₄ cups dried cranberries

²/₃ cup coarsely chopped white chocolate

DIRECTIONS

1. Preheat oven to 375°F (190°C).

2. In a medium bowl, cream together the butter and brown sugar until light and fluffy. Beat in the eggs one at a time. Combine oats, flour, salt, and baking soda; stir into butter mixture one cup at a time, mixing well after each addition. Stir in dried cranberries and white chocolate. Drop by rounded teaspoons onto ungreased cookie sheets.

3. Bake for 10 to 12 minutes in preheated oven, or until golden brown. Cool on wire racks.

Aaron's Chocolate Chunk Oatmeal Cookies

Submitted by: **Amanda Gladden**

Makes: 2 dozen
Preparation: 5 minutes
Cooking: 10 minutes
Total: 30 minutes

"This recipe is very fast and easy. The white cake mix, butterscotch pudding, and sour cream make these cookies rich and unique, and the recipe takes only 5 minutes to make! My boyfriend loves them."

INGREDIENTS

1 (18.25 ounce) package white cake mix

1 (3.5 ounce) package instant butterscotch pudding mix

⅔ cup rolled oats

½ cup vegetable oil

½ cup sour cream

¼ cup water

2 teaspoons vanilla extract

1 cup semisweet chocolate chips

DIRECTIONS

1. Preheat oven to 350°F (175°C). Lightly grease cookie sheets.

2. In a large bowl, stir together cake mix, instant pudding, and rolled oats. Add oil, sour cream, water, and vanilla; mix until smooth and well blended. Stir in chocolate chips. Roll dough into 1½ inch balls, and place 2 inches apart on the prepared cookie sheets.

3. Bake for 8 to 10 minutes in the preheated oven. Allow cookies to cool on baking sheet for 5 minutes before transferring to a wire rack to cool completely.

Chewy Chocolate Chip Oatmeal Cookies

Submitted by: **Dr Amy**

Makes: 3½ dozen

Preparation: 15 minutes

Cooking: 12 minutes

Total: 55 minutes

"I modified Beatrice's Excellent Oatmeal cookies very slightly. I came up with something that my boyfriend went CRAZY over! I've never seen him enjoy cookies to that extent! He said I blew his mother's recipe away."

INGREDIENTS

1 cup butter, softened

1 cup packed light brown sugar

½ cup white sugar

2 eggs

2 teaspoons vanilla extract

1¼ cups all-purpose flour

½ teaspoon baking soda

1 teaspoon salt

3 cups quick-cooking oats

1 cup chopped walnuts

1 cup semisweet chocolate chips

DIRECTIONS

1. Preheat the oven to 325°F (165°C).

2. In a large bowl, cream together the butter, brown sugar, and white sugar until smooth. Beat in eggs one at a time, then stir in vanilla. Combine the flour, baking soda, and salt; stir into the creamed mixture until just blended. Mix in the quick oats, walnuts, and chocolate chips. Drop by heaping spoonfuls onto ungreased baking sheets.

3. Bake for 12 minutes in the preheated oven. Allow cookies to cool on baking sheet for 5 minutes before transferring to a wire rack to cool completely.

White Chocolate-Macadamia Nut Oatmeal Cookies

Makes: 4 dozen cookies

Preparation: 20 minutes

Cooking: 12 minutes

Total: 1 hour

Submitted by: **Holly**

"Oatmeal cookies are so tasty and this combination is a real treat! For crisper cookies, bake longer. If you leave the cookies on the cookie sheet for a few minutes before removing to cool to wire racks you will have a softer bottomed cookie."

INGREDIENTS

½ cup butter, softened

½ cup white sugar

½ cup packed brown sugar

1 egg

1 teaspoon vanilla extract

1½ cups all-purpose flour

1 teaspoon baking powder

1 teaspoon baking soda

1½ cups rolled oats

1 cup chopped white chocolate

1 cup chopped macadamia nuts

DIRECTIONS

1. Preheat oven to 350°F (175°C). Grease cookie sheets.

2. In a large bowl, cream together the butter, white sugar, and brown sugar until smooth. Beat in the egg, then stir in the vanilla. Combine the flour, baking powder, and baking soda; stir into the creamed mixture. Mix in the oats, white chocolate, and macadamia nuts until evenly distributed. Drop by teaspoonfuls onto the prepared cookie sheets.

3. Bake for 10 to 12 minutes in the preheated oven, or until edges are toasted. For crisper cookies, bake longer. If you leave the cookies on the cookie sheet for a few minutes before transferring to cool on wire racks you will have a softer bottomed cookie.

Butterscotch Oatmeal Cookies

Submitted by: **N. Michno**

Makes: 3 dozen

Preparation: 15 minutes

Cooking: 10 minutes

Total: 40 minutes

"A chewy oatmeal cookie with butterscotch chips and chocolate chips. Nuts also taste good."

INGREDIENTS

3/4 cup butter flavored shortening

1/2 cup white sugar

1 cup packed brown sugar

1 egg

1 teaspoon vanilla extract

1 cup all-purpose flour

1 teaspoon baking soda

3 cups rolled oats

1 cup semisweet chocolate chips

1 cup butterscotch chips

DIRECTIONS

1. Preheat oven to 375°F (190°C).

2. In a large bowl, cream together shortening, white sugar, and brown sugar until smooth. Beat in egg, then stir in vanilla. Combine flour and baking soda, and mix into the batter. Mix in oats and chocolate and butterscotch chips. Drop dough by teaspoonfuls onto ungreased cookie sheets.

3. Bake for 9 to 12 minutes in the preheated oven, or until the edges are toasted. Cool on wire racks.

Coconut Oatmeal Cookies II

Submitted by: **Claire Kalpakjian**

Makes: 2 dozen

Preparation: 15 minutes

Cooking: 10 minutes

Total: 40 minutes

"This is a variation on a traditional oatmeal cookie. The white chocolate is a delicate touch to a rich, delicious cookie. Enjoy!"

INGREDIENTS

1¼ cups butter, softened

¾ cup packed brown sugar

½ cup white sugar

1 egg

1 teaspoon vanilla extract

1½ cups all-purpose flour

1 teaspoon baking soda

2½ cups rolled oats

¾ cup flaked coconut

1 cup white chocolate chips

DIRECTIONS

1. Preheat oven to 350°F (175°C).

2. In a medium bowl, cream together butter, brown sugar, and white sugar. Mix in the egg and vanilla. Combine flour and baking soda; blend into creamed mixture. Stir in the rolled oats, coconut, and white chocolate chips. Drop dough by rounded tablespoons onto ungreased cookie sheets.

3. Bake for 10 to 12 minutes in preheated oven, or until lightly browned. Cool on wire racks.

Cowboy Oatmeal Cookies

Submitted by: **Ellie Davies**

Makes: 3 dozen

Preparation: 15 minutes

Cooking: 10 minutes

Total: 40 minutes

"It's a great cookie, one of the kids favorites. This doesn't call for nuts, but I sometimes add about 1/2 cup-chopped."

INGREDIENTS

2 cups all-purpose flour

½ teaspoon baking powder

1 teaspoon baking soda

½ teaspoon salt

½ cup margarine

½ cup vegetable oil

1 cup packed brown sugar

1 cup white sugar

2 eggs

2 cups quick cooking oats

1 cup butterscotch chips

DIRECTIONS

1. Preheat the oven to 350°F (175°C). Sift together flour, baking powder, baking soda, and salt; set aside.

2. In a medium bowl, cream margarine, oil, brown sugar, and white sugar until smooth. Beat in eggs one at a time. Gradually stir in the sifted ingredients until well blended. Mix in oats and butterscotch chips. Drop from a teaspoon onto ungreased cookie sheets.

3. Bake for 10 to 12 minutes in preheated oven, or until edges are golden. Let set up on the cookie sheets for a few minutes before transferring to wire racks to cool completely.

Cowboy Cookies III

Submitted by: **Bonnie Smith**

Makes: 5 dozen

Preparation: 15 minutes

Cooking: 10 minutes

Total: 1 hour

"These are yummy. If you can manage to get them to cook just the right way, they aren't crunchy, but soft and the tiniest bit chewy, and melt in your mouth!"

INGREDIENTS

2 cups all-purpose flour

1 teaspoon baking powder

1 teaspoon baking soda

1/2 teaspoon salt

1 cup butter, softened

1 cup white sugar

1 cup packed brown sugar

2 eggs

1 teaspoon vanilla extract

2 cups rolled oats

1 cup semisweet chocolate chips

DIRECTIONS

1. Preheat oven to 350°F (175°C). Grease baking sheets. Sift together the flour, baking powder, baking soda, and salt. Set aside.

2. In a large bowl, cream together the butter, white sugar, and brown sugar until light and fluffy. Beat in the eggs one at a time, then stir in the vanilla. Gradually stir in the sifted ingredients. Stir in the rolled oats and chocolate chips. Drop by rounded teaspoonfuls onto the prepared baking sheets.

3. Bake for 8 to 10 minutes in the preheated oven. Allow cookies to cool on baking sheets for 5 minutes before removing.

Colossal Cookies

Submitted by: **Judy**

Makes: 4 dozen

Preparation: 15 minutes

Cooking: 12 minutes

Total: 1 hour

"A large, chewy, chocolate chip, oatmeal, and peanut butter cookie."

INGREDIENTS

½ cup margarine, softened

1½ cups white sugar

1½ cups packed brown sugar

4 eggs

1 teaspoon vanilla extract

1 (16 ounce) jar crunchy peanut butter

2½ teaspoons baking soda

6 cups quick cooking oats

1 cup semisweet chocolate chips

DIRECTIONS

1. Preheat oven to 350°F (175°C).

2. In a large bowl, cream together the margarine, white sugar, and brown sugar until smooth. Beat in the eggs one at a time, then stir in the vanilla and peanut butter. Mix in the baking soda, oats, and chocolate chips until well blended. Drop ¼ cupfuls of dough 4 inches apart onto ungreased cookie sheets. Flatten with a fork to 2½ inches in diameter.

3. Bake for 10 to 12 minutes in preheated oven. Cool 1 minute on cookie sheet before transferring to wire racks to cool completely.

Monster Cookies II

Submitted by: **Lori Douglas**

Makes: 6 dozen

Preparation: 20 minutes

Cooking: 15 minutes

Total: 1 hour 45 minutes

"This recipe makes large cookies and has NO flour. I got it from my aunt in Southern Alberta (Canada) several years ago!! Hope you enjoy it."

INGREDIENTS

1 cup margarine, softened

2 cups white sugar

2 cups packed brown sugar

3 cups peanut butter

6 eggs

1½ teaspoons corn syrup

1½ teaspoons vanilla extract

4 teaspoons baking soda

9 cups rolled oats

½ pound candy-coated milk chocolate pieces

½ pound semisweet chocolate chips

DIRECTIONS

1. Preheat oven to 350°F (175°C).

2. In a large bowl, cream together the margarine, white sugar, brown sugar, and peanut butter until smooth. Beat in the eggs, two at a time, then stir in the corn syrup and vanilla. Mix in baking soda and oats until well blended. Stir in the chocolate candies and chocolate chips. Roll dough into 2 inch balls, and place 3 inches apart on an ungreased cookie sheet. Flatten slightly with a fork.

3. Bake for 12 to 15 minutes in the preheated oven. Cool on cookie sheets for a few minutes, before transferring to wire racks to cool completely.

Dishpan Cookies II

Submitted by: **Laura and Tammy**

Makes: 6 dozen

Preparation: 25 minutes

Cooking: 10 minutes

Total: 1 hour 25 minutes

"These cookies have a little of everything in them, except for a dishpan."

INGREDIENTS

2 cups margarine

2 cups white sugar

2 cups packed brown sugar

4 eggs

4 cups all-purpose flour

2 teaspoons baking soda

1 teaspoon baking powder

1 teaspoon salt

4 cups cornflakes cereal

1½ cups rolled oats

2 cups flaked coconut

3 cups semisweet chocolate chips

DIRECTIONS

1. Preheat oven to 350°F (175°C).

2. In a large bowl, cream together the margarine, brown sugar, and white sugar until smooth. Beat in the eggs one at a time, mixing well after each addition. Sift together the flour, baking soda, baking powder, and salt; stir into the creamed mixture until just blended. Then mix in the corn flakes cereal, rolled oats, coconut, and chocolate chips. Drop by heaping spoonfuls onto ungreased cookie sheets.

3. Bake for 8 to 10 minutes in the preheated oven, or until edges are lightly browned. Cool on wire racks.

Joey's Peanut Butter Cookies

Submitted by: **P.L. Weiss**

Makes: 3 dozen

Preparation: 15 minutes

Cooking: 10 minutes

Total: 1 hour

"My boyfriend's special recipe makes the peanut butteriest tasting cookie I have ever tasted. These soft and chewy peanut buttery cookies are the best!"

INGREDIENTS

1 cup peanut butter

1/2 cup butter, softened

1/2 cup white sugar

1/2 cup packed brown sugar

1 egg

3 tablespoons milk

1 teaspoon vanilla extract

1 1/4 cups all-purpose flour

3/4 teaspoon baking powder

1/4 teaspoon salt

DIRECTIONS

1. Preheat oven to 375 °F (190°C).

2. In a large bowl, cream together the peanut butter, butter, white sugar, and brown sugar until well blended. Beat in the egg, milk, and vanilla one at a time. Combine the flour, baking powder, and salt; stir into creamed mixture. Roll tablespoonfuls of dough into balls. Place cookies 2 inches apart onto ungreased cookie sheets. Press each ball once with fork tines.

3. Bake for 8 to 10 minutes in the preheated oven, or until edges are lightly browned.

Delicious Peanut Butter Cookies

Submitted by: **Carla Maenius**

Makes: 4 dozen

Preparation: 10 minutes

Cooking: 10 minutes

Total: 40 minutes

"I've tried many different peanut butter cookie recipes but my family still likes this one the best!"

INGREDIENTS

½ cup shortening

1¼ cups packed light brown sugar

¾ cup peanut butter

1 egg

3 tablespoons milk

1 tablespoon vanilla extract

1¾ cups all-purpose flour

¾ teaspoon baking soda

¾ teaspoon salt

DIRECTIONS

1. Preheat the oven to 375°F (190°C).

2. In a medium bowl, cream together shortening, brown sugar, and peanut butter until smooth. Stir in egg, milk, and vanilla. Combine flour, baking soda, and salt; stir into the peanut butter mixture until well blended. Drop by rounded spoonfuls onto ungreased cookie sheets.

3. Bake for 8 to 10 minutes in the preheated oven. Allow cookies to cool on baking sheet for 5 minutes before transferring to a wire rack to cool completely.

Peanut Butter Cookies II

Submitted by: **Carol**

Makes: 6 dozen

Preparation: 15 minutes

Cooking: 15 minutes

Total: 1 hour 20 minutes

"These cookies are a favorite among children as well as adults and seem to be one of my children's favorites."

INGREDIENTS

1 cup butter, softened

1 cup white sugar

1 cup packed brown sugar

2 eggs

1 cup peanut butter

2 cups all-purpose flour

2 teaspoons baking soda

1/4 teaspoon salt

1 cup flaked coconut

DIRECTIONS

1. Preheat oven to 375°F (190°C).

2. In a medium bowl, cream together the butter, white sugar, and brown sugar until light and fluffy. Beat in the eggs one at a time, then mix in the peanut butter. Combine the flour, baking soda, and salt; blend in to form a soft dough. Mix in coconut. Drop dough by teaspoonfuls onto ungreased cookie sheets. Flatten each cookie using the tines of a fork.

3. Bake for 12 to 15 minutes in the preheated oven. Cool on wire racks.

Peanut Butter Cookies IV

Submitted by: **Linda White**

Makes: 4 dozen

Preparation: 20 minutes

Cooking: 12 minutes

Total: 1 hour

"Very delicious cookies. Easy to make. These will stay soft in an air-tight container. For special occasions, press five peanut halves into the top."

INGREDIENTS

1 1/4 cups sifted all-purpose flour

3/4 teaspoon baking soda

1/4 teaspoon salt

1/2 cup butter

1/2 cup peanut butter

1/2 cup white sugar

1/2 cup packed brown sugar

1 egg

1/2 teaspoon vanilla extract

1/2 cup white sugar for decoration

DIRECTIONS

1. Preheat the oven to 375°F (190°C). Sift together flour, baking soda, and salt; set aside.

2. In a medium bowl, cream together butter, peanut butter, 1/2 cup white sugar, and brown sugar until smooth. Beat in egg, then stir in vanilla. Gradually blend in the sifted ingredients. Shape dough into 1 inch balls. Roll in remaining sugar. Place 2 inches apart on ungreased cookie sheets. Criss-cross with fork tines.

3. Bake at for 10 to 12 minutes in the preheated oven. Cool slightly, and remove from pan.

Quick Peanut Butter Cookies

Submitted by: **Vicki Douglas**

Makes: 3 dozen

Preparation: 15 minutes

Cooking: 8 minutes

Total: 40 minutes

"I had to make cookies at the last minute for a school function and a friend gave me this quick and easy recipe. From start to finish, this only takes about 30-45 minutes and the taste is like you spent hours in the kitchen. You might want to make a double batch, because they will be gone before you know it. ENJOY!!"

INGREDIENTS

1 cup peanut butter

1 cup white sugar

1 egg

1 teaspoon baking soda

DIRECTIONS

1. Preheat oven to 325°F (165°C).

2. In a medium bowl, mix together the peanut butter, sugar, egg, and baking soda until well blended. Roll dough into 1 inch balls, and place on ungreased cookie sheets.

3. Bake for 6 to 8 minutes in the preheated oven. Cool on cookie sheets until set, before transferring to wire racks to cool completely.

Uncle Mac's Peanut Butter and Jelly Cookies

Makes: 12 cookies

Preparation: 20 minutes

Cooking: 10 minutes

Total: 30 minutes

Submitted by: **Edie Hathaway**

"Soft, tasty peanut butter cookies with a touch of jelly on top. No flour needed."

INGREDIENTS

1 cup peanut butter

1 cup white sugar

1 egg

1 teaspoon vanilla extract

2 tablespoons fruit preserves, any flavor

DIRECTIONS

1. Preheat oven to 350°F (175°C).

2. In a medium bowl, mix together peanut butter, sugar, egg, and vanilla until well blended. Drop by teaspoonfuls onto ungreased cookie sheets. Use a fork to make a criss-cross pattern on the top. Make a small hole in the top of each cookie using the handle of a wooden spoon. Fill the holes with preserves.

3. Bake for 8 to 11 minutes in preheated oven. Allow to cool for a couple of minutes on the cookie sheets before transferring to wire racks to cool completely.

Elaine's Peanut Butter Cookies

Submitted by: **Janet Kay**

Makes: 3 dozen

Preparation: 10 minutes

Cooking: 12 minutes

Total: 45 minutes

"This is a quick recipe for cookies when you are in a crunch for time and need to have something for the dessert platter now! These are very soft and taste great. I have yet to have anyone toss these cookies back on my platter."

INGREDIENTS

1 (18.5 ounce) package yellow cake mix

1 cup creamy peanut butter

½ cup vegetable oil

2 eggs

2 tablespoons water

DIRECTIONS

1. Preheat oven to 350°F (175°C).

2. Pour the cake mix into a large bowl. Make a well in the center, and add peanut butter, oil, eggs, and water. Mix until well blended. Drop by teaspoonfuls onto ungreased cookie sheets. Flatten slightly using a fork dipped in water.

3. Bake for 10 to 12 minutes in the preheated oven. Let cookies set on cookie sheet for 2 to 3 minutes before carefully removing from the cookie sheet to cool on wire racks.

Oatmeal Peanut Butter Cookies

Submitted by: **Michele**

Makes: 4 dozen

Preparation: 15 minutes

Cooking: 15 minutes

Total: 1 hour

"A nice change of pace from the usual peanut butter cookie. My husband never liked peanut butter cookies until I made him this recipe."

INGREDIENTS

½ cup shortening

½ cup margarine, softened

1 cup packed brown sugar

¾ cup white sugar

1 cup peanut butter

2 eggs

1½ cups all-purpose flour

2 teaspoons baking soda

1 teaspoon salt

1 cup quick-cooking oats

DIRECTIONS

1. Preheat oven to 350°F (175°C).

2. In a large bowl, cream together shortening, margarine, brown sugar, white sugar, and peanut butter until smooth. Beat in the eggs one at a time until well blended. Combine the flour, baking soda, and salt; stir into the creamed mixture. Mix in the oats until just combined. Drop by teaspoonfuls onto ungreased cookie sheets.

3. Bake for 10 to 15 minutes in the preheated oven, or until just light brown. Don't over-bake. Cool and store in an airtight container.

Chocolate Peanut Butter Cup Cookies

Submitted by: **Joanna Knudsen**

Makes: 3 dozen

Preparation: 15 minutes

Cooking: 10 minutes

Total: 1 hour 10 minutes

"These are THE BEST cookies I have ever eaten. They are a definite hit. If you like peanut butter and chocolate - these cookies are for you!"

INGREDIENTS

1 cup butter, softened

3/4 cup creamy peanut butter

3/4 cup white sugar

3/4 cup packed brown sugar

2 eggs

1 teaspoon vanilla extract

2 1/3 cups all-purpose flour

1/3 cup cocoa powder

1 teaspoon baking soda

1 cup semisweet chocolate chips

1 cup peanut butter chips

10 chocolate covered peanut butter cups, cut into eighths

DIRECTIONS

1. Preheat oven to 350°F (175°C).

2. In a large bowl, cream together the butter, peanut butter, white sugar, and brown sugar until smooth. Beat in the eggs one at a time, then stir in the vanilla. Combine the flour, cocoa, and baking soda; stir into the peanut butter mixture. Mix in the chocolate chips, peanut butter chips, and peanut butter cups. Drop by tablespoonfuls onto ungreased cookie sheets.

3. Bake for 8 to 10 minutes in the preheated oven. Let cool for 1 or 2 minutes on sheet before removing, or they will fall apart.

Chewy Peanut Butter Chocolate Chip Cookies

Submitted by: **Kathy Bliesner**

Makes: 2 dozen

Preparation: 15 minutes

Cooking: 15 minutes

Total: 1 hour

"These cookies are really chewy and addictive."

INGREDIENTS

½ cup butter, softened

½ cup peanut butter

1 cup packed brown sugar

½ cup white sugar

2 eggs

2 tablespoons light corn syrup

2 tablespoons water

2 teaspoons vanilla extract

2½ cups all-purpose flour

1 teaspoon baking soda

½ teaspoon salt

2 cups chopped semisweet chocolate

DIRECTIONS

1. Preheat oven to 375°F (190°C).

2. In a large bowl, cream together the butter, peanut butter, brown sugar, and white sugar until smooth. Beat in the eggs one at a time, then stir in the corn syrup, water, and vanilla. Combine the flour, baking soda, and salt; stir into the peanut butter mixture. Fold in chocolate chunks. Drop by ¼ cupfuls 3 inches apart onto ungreased baking sheets.

3. Bake for 12 to 14 minutes in the preheated oven, or until edges are golden. Allow cookies to cool for 1 minute on the cookie sheet before removing to wire racks to cool completely.

Peanut Butter Candy Blossoms

Submitted by: **Carole Zee**

Makes: 20 cookies

Preparation: 30 minutes

Cooking: 15 minutes

Total: 2 hours

"Friend gave this to me a long time ago."

INGREDIENTS

1 cup butter, softened

1 cup creamy peanut butter

1 cup packed brown sugar

1 cup white sugar

2 eggs

1 teaspoon vanilla extract

2$1/2$ cups all-purpose flour

1 teaspoon baking soda

$1/2$ teaspoon salt

20 fun size bars chocolate covered peanut nougat (e.g. Snickers®), unwrapped

DIRECTIONS

1. In a large bowl, cream together the butter, peanut butter, brown sugar, and white sugar until smooth. Beat in the eggs and vanilla. Stir in the flour, baking soda and salt until well blended. Cover and chill dough for at least one hour, or until no longer sticky.

2. Preheat the oven to 350°F (175°C). Take about $1/3$ cup of the dough, and wrap it around a candy bar. Repeat, using the rest of the dough and candy bars. Place cookies 3 inches apart onto ungreased cookie sheets.

3. Bake for 15 minutes in the preheated oven, or until edges begin to brown. Cool on baking sheets.

Aunt Cora's World's Greatest Cookies

Submitted by: **Mary Hays**

Makes: 4 dozen

Preparation: 15 minutes

Cooking: 15 minutes

Total: 1 hour 45 minutes

"Aunt Cora's recipe. WORLD'S BEST CHOCOLATE CHIP PEANUT BUTTER COOKIES!"

INGREDIENTS

1 cup margarine, softened

1 cup peanut butter

1 cup white sugar

1 cup packed brown sugar

2 eggs

2 cups unbleached all-purpose flour

1 teaspoon baking soda

2 cups semisweet chocolate chips

DIRECTIONS

1. Preheat oven to 325°F (165°C).

2. In a large bowl, cream together the margarine, peanut butter, white sugar, and brown sugar until smooth. Beat in the eggs one at a time, mixing well after each. Combine the flour and baking soda; stir into the peanut butter mixture. Mix in chocolate chips. Drop by heaping spoonfuls onto ungreased cookie sheets.

3. Bake for 12 to 15 minutes in the preheated oven, or until lightly browned at the edges. Allow cookies to cool on the cookie sheets for a minute before removing to wire racks to cool completely.

Cocoa Quickies

Submitted by: **Diana Lawton**

"Really good! I know the recipe by heart!"

Makes: 1 1/2 dozen

Preparation: 15 minutes

Total: 1 hour 15 minutes

INGREDIENTS

1/2 cup milk

1/2 cup butter

2 cups white sugar

6 tablespoons unsweetened cocoa powder

3 cups rolled oats

1 cup shredded coconut (optional)

DIRECTIONS

1. Place the milk, butter, sugar, and cocoa in a medium sized saucepan, and bring to a full rolling boil. Boil for one minute. Remove from heat, and stir in oats. Mix in coconut, if desired. Drop by teaspoonfuls onto waxed paper. Let stand until set. Quickies may be refrigerated to speed setting.

No Bake Cookies

Submitted by: **Denise**

Makes: 3 dozen

Preparation: 10 minutes

Total: 45 minutes

"Tasty no-bake cookies made with oatmeal, peanut butter and cocoa. Start timing when mixture reaches a full rolling boil; this is the trick to successful cookies. If you boil too long the cookies will be dry and crumbly. If you don't boil long enough, the cookies won't form properly."

INGREDIENTS

1¾ cups white sugar

½ cup milk

½ cup butter

4 tablespoons unsweetened cocoa powder

½ cup crunchy peanut butter

3 cups quick-cooking oats

1 teaspoon vanilla extract

DIRECTIONS

1. In a medium saucepan, combine sugar, milk, butter, and cocoa. Bring to a boil, and cook for 1½ minutes. Remove from heat, and stir in peanut butter, oats, and vanilla. Drop by teaspoonfuls onto wax paper. Let cool until hardened.

Peanut Butter Chews

Submitted by: **Cindy**

Makes: 3 dozen

Preparation: 25 minutes

Total: 55 minutes

"The peanut butter chews that were sold in school cafeterias. I make these for my kids all the time, and sometimes drizzle chocolate and butterscotch on top of the cookies. Rich, but excellent!"

INGREDIENTS

1 cup corn syrup

1 cup white sugar

1 cup creamy peanut butter

4$1/2$ cups cornflakes cereal

1 cup semi-sweet chocolate chips (optional)

1 cup butterscotch chips (optional)

DIRECTIONS

1. In a large saucepan over medium heat, combine corn syrup and white sugar. Bring to a boil, boil for one minute, and remove from heat. Stir in peanut butter until well blended. Mix in cereal until evenly coated. Drop by spoonfuls onto waxed paper.

2. In a glass bowl in the microwave, or using a double boiler, melt chocolate chips and butterscotch chips, stirring frequently until smooth. Drizzle on the top of the cookies.

143

No Bake Cookies IV

Submitted by: **Lisa**

Makes: 3 dozen

Preparation: 20 minutes

Total: 50 minutes

"Chocolate chips, oatmeal, peanut butter, marshmallows. No baking, just drop onto waxed paper, and place in refrigerator to set."

INGREDIENTS

1 cup semisweet chocolate chips

1/3 cup butter

16 large marshmallows

1/3 cup creamy peanut butter

1/2 teaspoon vanilla extract

1 cup flaked coconut

2 cups rolled oats

DIRECTIONS

1. In the top half of a double boiler, melt chocolate chips, butter, and marshmallows over low heat. Stir until smooth, and remove from heat. Stir in the peanut butter, vanilla, coconut, and oats. Mix thoroughly. Drop by rounded spoonfuls onto waxed paper. Refrigerate for about 30 minutes, or until set.

spice cookies

A cold winter day is instantly transformed into cozy comfort with a big, soft molasses cookie and a hot cup of tea. A summer's day is quickly cooled with a crisp ginger snap and an ice-cold glass of lemonade. The holidays are even more festive with gingerbread men smiling up from a silver tray. Ginger, nutmeg, cloves, and cinnamon make cookies for all seasons.

Grammy Burnham's Molasses Cookies

Submitted by: **Hazel Fritz**

Makes: 3 dozen

Preparation: 15 minutes

Cooking: 15 minutes

Total: 45 minutes

"A batch of these soft cookies is always a yummy treat!"

INGREDIENTS

½ cup shortening

1½ cups white sugar

3 eggs

½ cup molasses

2¾ cups all-purpose flour

1 teaspoon baking soda

1 teaspoon ground cinnamon

1 teaspoon ground allspice

1 teaspoon ground ginger

1½ cups raisins

DIRECTIONS

1. Preheat oven to 350°F (175°C). Grease baking sheets.

2. In a large bowl, cream together shortening and sugar until smooth. Beat in the eggs one at a time, then stir in the molasses. Combine the flour, baking soda, cinnamon, allspice, and ginger; blend into the molasses mixture. Stir in raisins. Drop dough by tablespoonfuls onto prepared baking sheets.

3. Bake for 12 to 15 minutes in preheated oven, or until the center is set. Cool on wire racks.

Soft Molasses Cookies II

Submitted by: **Anna S. Uhland**

Makes: 5 dozen

Preparation: 15 minutes

Cooking: 12 minutes

Total: 55 minutes

"The best soft molasses cookie I've ever eaten! You may substitute 3/4 cup undiluted evaporated milk with 3/4 tablespoon vinegar for the sour cream. Cookies can be iced with a mixture of confectioners' sugar and milk, or just sprinkled with confectioners' sugar."

INGREDIENTS

3 cups sifted all-purpose flour

2 teaspoons baking soda

1 teaspoon salt

1 teaspoon ground ginger

1 teaspoon ground cinnamon

1 cup butter

1 cup white sugar

1 egg

1/3 cup molasses

3/4 cup sour cream

DIRECTIONS

1. Preheat oven to 375°F (190°C). Sift together flour, baking soda, salt, ginger, and cinnamon; set aside.

2. Cream butter, and gradually blend in sugar until light and fluffy. Beat in egg and molasses. Mix in sour cream alternately with sifted dry ingredients. Drop dough by teaspoonfuls onto ungreased cookie sheets.

3. Bake 10 to 12 minutes in preheated oven. Transfer to wire racks to cool.

Mom's Ginger Snaps

Submitted by: **Elaine**

Makes: 3 dozen

Preparation: 15 minutes

Cooking: 12 minutes

Total: 40 minutes

"Fabulous, spicy cookies."

INGREDIENTS

1 cup packed brown sugar

3/4 cup vegetable oil

1/4 cup molasses

1 egg

2 cups all-purpose flour

2 teaspoons baking soda

1/4 teaspoon salt

1/2 teaspoon ground cloves

1 teaspoon ground cinnamon

1 teaspoon ground ginger

1/3 cup white sugar for decoration

DIRECTIONS

1. Preheat oven to 375°F (190°C).

2. In a large bowl, mix together the brown sugar, oil, molasses, and egg. Combine the flour, baking soda, salt, cloves, cinnamon, and ginger; stir into the molasses mixture. Roll dough into 1¼ inch balls. Roll each ball in white sugar before placing 2 inches apart on ungreased cookie sheets.

3. Bake for 10 to 12 minutes in preheated oven, or until center is firm. Cool on wire racks.

Big Soft Ginger Cookies

Submitted by: **Amy Sacha**

Makes: 2 dozen

Preparation: 15 minutes

Cooking: 10 minutes

Total: 50 minutes

"These are just what they say: big, soft, gingerbread cookies. They stay soft, too. My oldest son's favorite."

INGREDIENTS

2¼ cups all-purpose flour

2 teaspoons ground ginger

1 teaspoon baking soda

¾ teaspoon ground cinnamon

½ teaspoon ground cloves

¼ teaspoon salt

¾ cup margarine, softened

1 cup white sugar

1 egg

1 tablespoon water

¼ cup molasses

2 tablespoons white sugar

DIRECTIONS

1. Preheat oven to 350°F (175°C). Sift together the flour, ginger, baking soda, cinnamon, cloves, and salt. Set aside.

2. In a large bowl, cream together the margarine and 1 cup sugar until light and fluffy. Beat in the egg, then stir in the water and molasses. Gradually stir the sifted ingredients into the molasses mixture. Shape dough into walnut sized balls, and roll them in the remaining 2 tablespoons of sugar. Place the cookies 2 inches apart onto an ungreased cookie sheet, and flatten slightly.

3. Bake for 8 to 10 minutes in the preheated oven. Allow cookies to cool on baking sheet for 5 minutes before removing to a wire rack to cool completely. Store in an airtight container.

Joe Froggers

Submitted by: **Ingrid**

Makes: 4 dozen

Preparation: 15 minutes

Cooking: 12 minutes

Total: 10 hours

"A soft, dark, molasses-spice cookie. An old time American cookie from New England, attributed to the legendary "Uncle Joe" who made cookies as big as lily pads."

INGREDIENTS

½ cup shortening

1 cup white sugar

1 cup dark molasses

½ cup water

4 cups all-purpose flour

1½ teaspoons salt

1 teaspoon baking soda

1½ teaspoons ground ginger

½ teaspoon ground cloves

½ teaspoon ground nutmeg

¼ teaspoon ground allspice

DIRECTIONS

1. In a large bowl, cream shortening and sugar together. Mix in water and molasses. Sift together flour, salt, baking powder, ginger, cloves, nutmeg, allspice; blend into the shortening mixture. Cover, and chill overnight.

2. Preheat oven to 375 degrees F (190 degrees C). Lightly grease cookie sheets. Roll out cookie dough ¼ inch thick on floured surface. Cut with 3 inch cookie cutter, and arrange on prepared cookie sheets. Sprinkle cookies with additional sugar (optional).

3. Bake for 10 to 12 minutes. You need to leave cookies on cookie sheet for 2 minutes after baking to keep them from breaking.

Soft Gingerbread Cookies

Submitted by: **Sara**

Makes: 3 dozen

Preparation: 25 minutes

Cooking: 10 minutes

Total: 3 hours 45 minutes

"These cookies are warm and delicious on a cold winter's day. Cut them into any shape to fit your holiday celebrations."

INGREDIENTS

3/4 cup molasses

1/3 cup packed brown sugar

1/3 cup water

1/8 cup butter, softened

3 1/4 cups all-purpose flour

1 teaspoon baking soda

1/2 teaspoon ground allspice

1 teaspoon ground ginger

1/2 teaspoon ground cloves

1/2 teaspoon ground cinnamon

DIRECTIONS

1. In a medium bowl, mix together the molasses, brown sugar, water and butter until smooth. Combine the flour, baking soda, allspice, ginger, cloves and cinnamon, stir them into the wet mixture until all of the dry is absorbed. Cover the dough and chill for at least 3 hours.

2. Preheat oven to 350°F (175°C). On a lightly floured surface, roll the dough out to 1/4 inch thickness. Cut out into desired shapes. Place cookies 1 inch apart onto ungreased cookie sheets.

3. Bake for 8 to 10 minutes in the preheated oven. Remove from the cookie sheets to cool on wire racks.

Gingerbread Cookies

Submitted by: **Mary Beth Zabriskie**

Makes: 5 dozen

Preparation: 30 minutes

Cooking: 12 minutes

Total: 1 hour

"This is a wonderful recipe from Colonial Williamsburg."

INGREDIENTS

1 cup white sugar

2 teaspoons ground ginger

1 teaspoon ground nutmeg

1 teaspoon ground cinnamon

1/2 teaspoon salt

1 1/2 teaspoons baking soda

1 cup margarine, melted

1/2 cup evaporated milk

1 cup unsulfured molasses

3/4 teaspoon vanilla extract

3/4 teaspoon lemon extract

4 cups unbleached all-purpose flour

DIRECTIONS

1. Preheat oven to 375°F (190°C). Lightly grease cookie sheets.

2. In a large bowl, stir together the sugar, ginger, nutmeg, cinnamon, salt, and baking soda. Mix in the melted margarine, evaporated milk, molasses, vanilla, and lemon extracts. Stir in the flour, 1 cup at a time, mixing well after each addition. The dough should be stiff enough to handle without sticking to fingers. If necessary, increase flour by up to 1/2 cup to prevent sticking.

3. When the dough is smooth, roll it out to 1/4 inch thick on a floured surface, and cut into cookies. Place cookies on the prepared cookie sheets.

4. Bake for 10 to 12 minutes in the preheated oven. The cookies are done when the top springs back when touched. Remove from cookie sheets to cool on wire racks.

Gingerbread Cookies II

Submitted by: **Kim**

Makes: 6 dozen

Preparation: 20 minutes

Cooking: 12 minutes

Total: 4 hours

"This is the BEST recipe for gingerbread cookies I have ever tasted. It looks complicated, but isn't. I have used this recipe for many years and always get compliments on it."

INGREDIENTS

6 cups all-purpose flour

1 tablespoon baking powder

1 tablespoon ground ginger

1 teaspoon ground nutmeg

1 teaspoon ground cloves

1 teaspoon ground cinnamon

1 cup shortening, melted and cooled slightly

1 cup molasses

1 cup packed brown sugar

½ cup water

1 egg

1 teaspoon vanilla extract

DIRECTIONS

1. Sift together the flour, baking powder, ginger, nutmeg, cloves, and cinnamon; set aside.

2. In a medium bowl, mix together the shortening, molasses, brown sugar, water, egg, and vanilla until smooth. Gradually stir in the dry ingredients, until they are completely absorbed. Divide dough into 3 pieces, pat down to 1½ inch thickness, wrap in plastic wrap, and refrigerate for at least 3 hours.

3. Preheat oven to 350°F (175°C). On a lightly floured surface, roll the dough out to ¼ inch thickness. Cut into desired shapes with cookie cutters. Place cookies 1 inch apart onto an ungreased cookie sheet.

4. Bake for 10 to 12 minutes in the preheated oven. When the cookies are done, they will look dry, but still be soft to the touch. Remove from the baking sheet to cool on wire racks. When cool, the cookies can be frosted with the icing of your choice.

allrecipes tried & true cookies | spice cookies

155

Building Gingerbread

Submitted by: **Janice Brubaker**

Makes: 1 gingerbread house

Preparation: 30 minutes

Cooking: 15 minutes

Total: 3 hours

"Every Christmas I design a new pattern and make a gingerbread house for the holidays. The kids love to help decorate."

INGREDIENTS

5 cups all-purpose flour

1 teaspoon baking soda

1 teaspoon salt

1 teaspoon ground nutmeg

1 cup shortening

1 tablespoon ground ginger

1 cup white sugar

1 cup molasses

2½ cups confectioners' sugar

¼ teaspoon cream of tartar

2 egg whites

½ teaspoon vanilla extract

DIRECTIONS

1. Preheat the oven to 375°F (190°C).

2. Melt shortening in a saucepan large enough for mixing the dough. Mix in sugar and molasses. Combine the flour, salt, baking soda, nutmeg, and ginger; gradually stir into the pan, using your hands to work in the last bit. Dough should be stiff.

3. On a floured surface, roll out dough to ¼ inch thickness, and cut out as desired. Make sure the gingerbread is of uniform thickness, or the edges may burn before the center is done. Place pieces onto cookie sheets.

4. Bake for 13 to 15 minutes in the preheated oven. Let cool for several minutes on the cookie sheet, then remove to racks to finish cooling.

5. When the gingerbread has cooled completely, make the frosting cement. In a medium bowl, mix together confectioners' sugar and cream of tartar. Add egg whites and vanilla. Beat on high speed until frosting holds its shape. If necessary, add more confectioners' sugar to thicken the icing. Cover frosting with a damp cloth to prevent drying.

Iced Pumpkin Cookies

Submitted by: **Gina**

Makes: 3 dozen

Preparation: 20 minutes

Cooking: 20 minutes

Total: 1 hour 20 minutes

"Wonderful spicy iced pumpkin cookies that both kids and adults love!"

INGREDIENTS

2½ cups all-purpose flour

1 teaspoon baking powder

1 teaspoon baking soda

2 teaspoons ground cinnamon

½ teaspoon ground nutmeg

½ teaspoon ground cloves

½ teaspoon salt

½ cup butter, softened

1½ cups white sugar

1 cup canned pumpkin puree

1 egg

1 teaspoon vanilla extract

2 cups confectioners' sugar

3 tablespoons milk

1 tablespoon melted butter

1 teaspoon vanilla extract

DIRECTIONS

1. Preheat oven to 350°F (175°C). Combine flour, baking powder, baking soda, cinnamon, nutmeg, ground cloves, and salt; set aside.

2. In a medium bowl, cream together the ½ cup of butter and white sugar. Add pumpkin, egg, and 1 teaspoon vanilla to butter mixture, and beat until creamy. Mix in dry ingredients. Drop on cookie sheet by tablespoonfuls; flatten slightly.

3. Bake for 15 to 20 minutes in the preheated oven. Cool cookies, then drizzle glaze with fork.

4. To Make Glaze: Combine confectioners' sugar, milk, 1 tablespoon melted butter, and 1 teaspoon vanilla. Add milk as needed, to achieve drizzling consistency.

Pumpkin Cookies with Penuche Frosting

Submitted by: **Suzanne Stull**

Makes: 4 dozen

Preparation: 15 minutes

Cooking: 12 minutes

Total: 45 minutes

"A soft cookie with a candy frosting."

INGREDIENTS

1 cup shortening

½ cup packed brown sugar

½ cup white sugar

1 cup pumpkin puree

1 egg

1 teaspoon vanilla extract

2 cups all-purpose flour

1 teaspoon baking soda

1 teaspoon baking powder

1 teaspoon ground cinnamon

½ teaspoon salt

1 cup chopped walnuts

3 tablespoons butter

½ cup packed brown sugar

¼ cup milk

2 cups confectioners' sugar

DIRECTIONS

1. Preheat the oven to 350°F (175°C). Grease cookie sheets.

2. In a large bowl, cream together shortening, ½ cup brown sugar, and white sugar. Mix in pumpkin, egg, and vanilla. Sift together flour, baking soda, baking powder, cinnamon, and salt; mix into the creamed mixture. Stir in walnuts. Drop dough by heaping spoonfuls onto the prepared baking sheets.

3. Bake for 10 to 12 minutes in the preheated oven. Cool on wire racks.

4. In a small saucepan over medium heat, combine the 3 tablespoons butter and ½ cup brown sugar. Bring to a boil; cook and stir for 1 minute, or until slightly thickened. Cool slightly, then stir in the milk, and beat until smooth. Gradually stir in 2 cups confectioners' sugar until frosting has reached desired consistency. Spread on cooled cookies.

Pumpkin Cookies

Submitted by: **M.J.**

Makes: 3 dozen

Preparation: 15 minutes

Cooking: 10 minutes

Total: 35 minutes

"Yummy pumpkin cookies with spices and butterscotch morsels. Moist and delicious."

INGREDIENTS

½ cup shortening

1 cup white sugar

1 cup pumpkin puree

1 teaspoon vanilla extract

2 cups all-purpose flour

¼ teaspoon salt

1 teaspoon baking soda

1 teaspoon baking powder

1 teaspoon ground cinnamon

1½ cups butterscotch chips

DIRECTIONS

1. Preheat oven to 350°F (175°C). Grease cookie sheets.

2. In a medium bowl, cream the shortening and sugar. Stir in the pumpkin and vanilla. Sift together the flour, salt, baking soda, baking powder, and cinnamon; stir into the creamed mixture. Then mix in the butterscotch chips. Drop dough by teaspoonfuls onto the prepared cookie sheets.

3. Bake for 8 to 10 minutes in preheated oven. Allow cookies to cool for a minute on cookie sheets before transferring to wire cooling racks.

Pumpkin Chocolate Chip Cookies

Submitted by: **Beth**

Makes: 4 dozen

Preparation: 15 minutes

Cooking: 15 minutes

Total: 45 minutes

"You will be glad you tried this unique combination of nuts, chocolate, spices, and pumpkin."

INGREDIENTS

½ cup shortening

1½ cups white sugar

1 egg

1 cup canned pumpkin

1 teaspoon vanilla extract

2½ cups all-purpose flour

1 teaspoon baking powder

1 teaspoon baking soda

1 teaspoon salt

1 teaspoon ground nutmeg

1 teaspoon ground cinnamon

½ cup chopped walnuts (optional)

1 cup semisweet chocolate chips

DIRECTIONS

1. Preheat oven to 350°F (175°C). Grease cookie sheets.

2. In a large bowl, cream together the shortening and sugar until light and fluffy. Beat in the egg, then stir in the pumpkin and vanilla. Combine the flour, baking powder, baking soda, salt, nutmeg, and cinnamon; gradually mix into the creamed mixture. Stir in the walnuts and chocolate chips. Drop dough by teaspoonfuls onto the prepared cookie sheets.

3. Bake for 15 minutes in the preheated oven, or until light brown. Cool on wire racks.

Mrs. Sigg's Snickerdoodles

Submitted by: Beth Sigworth

Makes: 4 dozen

Preparation: 20 minutes

Cooking: 10 minutes

Total: 1 hour

"These wonderful cinnamon-sugar cookies became very popular with my friends at church. My pastor loves them! You will too! Crispy edges, and chewy centers; these cookies are a crowd pleaser for sure!"

INGREDIENTS

1/2 cup butter, softened

1/2 cup shortening

1 1/2 cups white sugar

2 eggs

2 teaspoons vanilla extract

2 3/4 cups all-purpose flour

2 teaspoons cream of tartar

1 teaspoon baking soda

1/4 teaspoon salt

2 tablespoons white sugar

2 teaspoons ground cinnamon

DIRECTIONS

1. Preheat oven to 400°F (200°C).

2. Cream together butter, shortening, 1 1/2 cups sugar, the eggs and the vanilla. Blend in the flour, cream of tartar, soda and salt. Shape dough by rounded spoonfuls into balls.

3. Mix the 2 tablespoons sugar and the cinnamon. Roll balls of dough in mixture. Place 2 inches apart on ungreased baking sheets.

4. Bake 8 to 10 minutes, or until set but not too hard. Remove immediately from baking sheets.

Ultimate Maple Snickerdoodles

Submitted by: **Linda Carroll**

Makes: 3 dozen

Preparation: 15 minutes

Cooking: 10 minutes

Total: 35 minutes

"These have been voted the number one cookie that I bake (and I bake a lot!), and are loved by all who eat them. They are chewy mapley good!"

INGREDIENTS

2 cups all-purpose flour

1½ teaspoons baking powder

¼ teaspoon baking soda

1½ teaspoons ground cinnamon

½ cup margarine, softened

1 cup white sugar

3 tablespoons real maple syrup

1 egg

½ cup white sugar

¼ cup maple sugar

DIRECTIONS

1. Preheat oven to 350°F (175°C). Stir together the flour, baking powder, baking soda, and cinnamon. Set aside.

2. In a large bowl, cream together the margarine and 1 cup of white sugar until light and fluffy. Beat in the egg and maple syrup. Gradually blend in the dry ingredients until just mixed. In a small dish, mix together the remaining ½ cup white sugar and the maple sugar. Roll dough into 1 inch balls, and roll the balls in the sugar mixture. Place cookies 2 inches apart on ungreased cookie sheets.

3. Bake 8 to 10 minutes in the preheated oven. Cookies will be crackly on top and look wet in the middle. Remove from cookie sheets to cool on wire racks.

Lighter Snickerdoodles

Submitted by: **Lisa**

Makes: 4 dozen

Preparation: 20 minutes

Cooking: 10 minutes

Total: 1 hour 50 minutes

"A less fattening version of an old favorite. Now you can eat even more!"

INGREDIENTS

¼ cup butter

1½ cups white sugar

4 ounces lowfat cream cheese

1 egg

2 egg whites

2¾ cups all-purpose flour

2 teaspoons cream of tartar

1 teaspoon baking soda

¼ teaspoon salt

¼ cup white sugar

2 teaspoons ground cinnamon

DIRECTIONS

1. In a large bowl, cream together the butter, 1½ cups of white sugar, and cream cheese. Beat in the egg and egg whites until smooth. Sift together the flour, cream of tartar, baking soda, and salt; stir into the creamed mixture. Cover, and refrigerate dough for at least 1 hour.

2. Preheat oven to 400°F (200°C). In a small dish, mix together the remaining white sugar and the cinnamon. Roll the dough into walnut sized balls, and roll the balls in the cinnamon and sugar mixture. Place the balls at least 2 inches apart on cookie sheets, and flatten slightly.

3. Bake for 8 to 10 minutes in the preheated oven. Remove from cookie sheets to cool on wire racks.

Cinnamon Sugar Cookies

Submitted by: **Holly**

Makes: 5 dozen

Preparation: 25 minutes

Cooking: 15 minutes

Total: 4 hours 45 minutes

"A traditional refrigerator cookie rolled in cinnamon sugar before baking. Great for making ahead of time."

INGREDIENTS

1¼ cups all-purpose flour

¼ teaspoon baking soda

¼ teaspoon salt

½ cup butter

¼ cup white sugar

¾ cup packed light brown sugar

1 egg

1 teaspoon vanilla extract

½ cup white sugar

2½ tablespoons ground cinnamon

DIRECTIONS

1. Sift together the flour, baking soda, and salt; set aside. In a medium bowl, cream butter with ¼ cup white sugar and brown sugar. Mix in egg and vanilla. Add the sifted dry ingredients, and mix until well blended. Divide dough into 3 equal portions. Roll into logs 2 inches in diameter, wrap, and refrigerate for 3 to 4 hours. These logs can be frozen for up to 6 weeks.

2. Preheat oven to 350°F (175°C). Mix ½ cup sugar and cinnamon on a flat plate or a piece of wax paper. Unwrap dough logs, and roll in the cinnamon mixture. Cut into ¼ inch slices, and place 2 inches apart onto ungreased cookie sheets.

3. Bake 12 to 15 minutes in the preheated oven. Remove from baking sheets to cool on wire racks. Baked cookies can be kept in an airtight container for up to 2 weeks.

Polvorones de Canele (Cinnamon Cookies)

Makes: 2 dozen

Preparation: 20 minutes

Cooking: 20 minutes

Total: 1 hour

Submitted by: **Cathy**

"A Mexican-style cookie rolled in cinnamon sugar."

INGREDIENTS

1 cup butter

½ cup confectioners' sugar

½ teaspoon ground cinnamon

¼ teaspoon salt

1 teaspoon vanilla extract

1½ cups all-purpose flour

1 cup confectioners' sugar

1 teaspoon ground cinnamon

DIRECTIONS

1. Preheat oven to 350°F (175°C). Grease cookie sheets.

2. In a medium bowl, cream together ½ cup confectioners' sugar and butter until smooth. Stir in vanilla. Combine flour, salt, and ½ teaspoon of cinnamon; stir into the creamed mixture to form a stiff dough. Shape dough into 1 inch balls. Mix together 1 cup confectioners' sugar and 1 teaspoon cinnamon; roll balls in cinnamon mixture.

3. Bake for 15 to 20 minutes in preheated oven, or until nicely browned. Cool cookies on wire racks.

Jumbo Raisin Cookies

Submitted by: **Mary Beth Zabriskie**

Makes: 2½ dozen

Preparation: 20 minutes

Cooking: 15 minutes

Total: 50 minutes

"Juicy raisins are the star in these popular cookies! They're great as a snack with coffee."

INGREDIENTS

2 cups raisins

1 cup water

3½ cups all-purpose flour

1 teaspoon baking powder

1 teaspoon baking soda

1 teaspoon salt

½ teaspoon ground cinnamon

½ teaspoon ground nutmeg

1 cup shortening

1¾ cups white sugar

2 eggs

1 teaspoon vanilla extract

½ cup chopped walnuts

DIRECTIONS

1. Place water and raisins in a small saucepan, and bring to boil. Boil 3 to 4 minutes. Set aside to cool.

2. Preheat oven to 375°F (190°C). Grease cookie sheets.

3. Combine flour, baking powder, baking soda, salt, cinnamon, and nutmeg; set aside.

4. In a large bowl, cream together shortening and sugar. Beat in eggs and vanilla. Stir in raisins along with the liquid in which they were boiled. Blend in flour mixture, then mix in the walnuts. Drop by tablespoonfuls onto the prepared cookie sheets.

5. Bake for 12 to 15 minutes in preheated oven, or until firm. Remove from cookie sheets to cool on wire racks.

Zucchini Nut Cookies

Submitted by: **Maureen Pruitt**

Makes: 3 dozen

Preparation: 15 minutes

Cooking: 15 minutes

Total: 1 hour

"This recipe makes a soft, spicy cookie with a nutty crunch!"

INGREDIENTS

½ cup packed brown sugar

½ cup white sugar

½ cup shortening

1 egg

2 cups sifted all-purpose flour

1 teaspoon baking soda

1 teaspoon ground cinnamon

½ teaspoon ground nutmeg

½ teaspoon ground cloves

¼ teaspoon salt

1 cup grated zucchini

1 cup raisins

½ cup chopped walnuts

DIRECTIONS

1. Preheat oven to 325°F (165°C). Grease cookie sheets.

2. Cream together shortening, brown sugar, and white sugar until smooth. Beat in egg. Combine the flour, baking soda, salt, cinnamon, nutmeg, and cloves; stir into the creamed mixture. Mix in zucchini, raisins, and walnuts. Drop by rounded tablespoons onto the prepared baking sheets.

3. Bake 15 minutes in the preheated oven, or until lightly browned. Cool on the cookie sheets for a few minutes before removing to wire racks to cool completely.

bar cookies

If you love squares of rich, gooey chocolate-upon-chocolate layers or chewy, fruity bursts of nutty goodness, then this chapter is for you! In the mood to drown your sorrows in a pan of brownies? Wish to surprise your friends with an elegant plate of lemon bars? Looking for a healthy but fun snack for the kids' lunches? Bar cookies are quick solutions for all of these dilemmas, and you'll find the best of the best on the following pages.

Best Brownies

Submitted by: **Angie**

"These brownies always turn out!"

Makes: 16 brownies

Preparation: 25 minutes

Cooking: 35 minutes

Total: 1 hour

INGREDIENTS

½ cup butter

1 cup white sugar

2 eggs

1 teaspoon vanilla extract

⅓ cup unsweetened cocoa powder

½ cup all-purpose flour

¼ teaspoon salt

¼ teaspoon baking powder

3 tablespoons butter, softened

3 tablespoons unsweetened cocoa powder

1 tablespoon honey

1 teaspoon vanilla extract

1 cup confectioners' sugar

DIRECTIONS

1. Preheat oven to 350°F (175°C). Grease and flour an 8 inch square pan.

2. In a large saucepan, melt ½ cup butter. Remove from heat, and stir in sugar, eggs, and 1 teaspoon vanilla. Beat in ⅓ cup cocoa, ½ cup flour, salt, and baking powder. Spread batter into prepared pan.

3. Bake in preheated oven for 25 to 30 minutes. Do not overcook.

4. To Make Frosting: Combine 3 tablespoons butter, 3 tablespoons cocoa, 1 tablespoon honey, 1 teaspoon vanilla, and 1 cup confectioners' sugar. Frost brownies while they are still warm.

Dump Bars

Submitted by: **Barb Lawrence**

Makes: 1 - 9x13 inch pan
Preparation: 15 minutes
Cooking: 35 minutes
Total: 50 minutes

"This is the most awesome brownie that I have ever tasted!"

INGREDIENTS

2 cups white sugar

5 eggs

1 cup vegetable oil

1 teaspoon vanilla extract

1⅓ cups all-purpose flour

½ cup unsweetened cocoa powder

1 teaspoon salt

1 cup semisweet chocolate chips

DIRECTIONS

1. Preheat oven to 350°F (175°C). Grease a 9x13 inch pan.

2. In a large bowl, stir together sugar, eggs, oil, and vanilla until well blended. Combine the flour, cocoa, and salt; mix into the egg mixture until just moistened. Spread the batter evenly into the prepared pan. Sprinkle chocolate chips over the top.

3. Bake for 30 to 35 minutes in preheated oven, or until brownies start to pull away from the sides of the pan. Allow to cool before cutting into squares.

Brownies To Die For

Submitted by: **V. Stogner**

Makes: 1 - 9x9 inch pan

Preparation: 15 minutes

Cooking: 35 minutes

Total: 50 minutes

"A luscious coconut, pecan, caramel, sour cream brownie that will have your taste buds dancing and begging for more. We have at times even melted caramels on top with the pecans instead of the chocolate chips, or have mixed caramels into the batter along with everything else. Your friends will demand the recipe."

INGREDIENTS

1 (19.8 ounce) package brownie mix

1 cup sour cream

1 (16 ounce) container coconut pecan frosting

1 cup semisweet chocolate chips

1 cup chopped pecans

DIRECTIONS

1. Preheat oven to 350°F (175°C). Grease one 9x9 inch baking pan.

2. Mix the brownie mix according to box directions, omitting ½ of the oil asked for. Stir in the sour cream and coconut pecan frosting. Spread evenly into the prepared pan.

3. Bake for 20 to 30 minutes in preheated oven. Be careful not to overbake, or they will harden and be impossible to eat! About 5 minutes before brownies are done, remove from oven, and sprinkle chocolate chips over the top along with chopped pecans. Place back in the oven for 5 minutes. Remove pan from oven, and use a spatula to spread the melted chocolate chips over the top to frost the brownies.

Bodacious Brownies

Submitted by: **Elizabeth**

Makes: 1 - 8x8 inch pan

Preparation: 15 minutes

Cooking: 25 minutes

Total: 40 minutes

"My kids love them, they all ways want me to make them. I drizzle them with melted chocolate and vanilla-flavored candy coating. Delicious!"

INGREDIENTS

$^1/_2$ cup butter or margarine

1 cup white sugar

$^1/_3$ cup unsweetened cocoa powder

2 eggs

1 teaspoon vanilla extract

1 cup all-purpose flour

$^3/_4$ teaspoon baking powder

$^1/_4$ teaspoon salt

$^1/_2$ cup chopped walnuts (optional)

DIRECTIONS

1. Preheat oven to 350°F (175°C). Grease an 8x8 inch baking pan.

2. Melt butter in medium sauce pan. Remove from heat, and stir in sugar and cocoa. Beat in the eggs one at a time, then stir in the vanilla. Combine the flour, baking powder, and salt; stir into the chocolate mixture until just blended. Fold in walnuts, if desired. Spread the batter evenly into the prepared pan.

3. Bake for 25 minutes in the preheated oven, or until a wooden pick inserted into the center comes out clean. Cool in pan on a wire rack.

Mmm-Mmm Better Brownies

Submitted by: **Sarah**

Makes: 1 9x9 inch pan

Preparation: 15 minutes

Cooking: 25 minutes

Total: 40 minutes

"I personally think these are the best brownies in the world. Try them, I think you'll agree! To make the brownies rich and buttery, use melted butter instead of the vegetable oil."

INGREDIENTS

½ cup vegetable oil

1 cup white sugar

1 teaspoon vanilla extract

2 eggs

½ cup all-purpose flour

⅓ cup unsweetened cocoa powder

¼ teaspoon baking powder

¼ teaspoon salt

½ cup chopped walnuts (optional)

DIRECTIONS

1. Preheat oven to 350°F (175°C). Grease a 9x9 inch baking pan.

2. In a medium bowl, mix together the oil, sugar, and vanilla. Beat in eggs. Combine flour, cocoa, baking powder, and salt; gradually stir into the egg mixture until well blended. Stir in walnuts, if desired. Spread the batter evenly into the prepared pan.

3. Bake for 20 to 25 minutes, or until the brownie begins to pull away from edges of pan. Let cool on a wire rack before cutting into squares.

Granny's Brownies

Submitted by: **Carl T. Erickson**

Makes: 1 - 8x8 inch pan
Preparation: 15 minutes
Cooking: 1 hour
Total: 1 hour 20 minutes

"This has been a recipe in our family since before the turn of the century. I am 70, so you can imagine when it started to get down to my sister and me. Now my grand-nephew enjoys them. Keep under lock and key, or they will disappear in a trice!"

INGREDIENTS

3/4 cup butter

2 cups packed brown sugar

3 eggs

4 (1 ounce) squares unsweetened chocolate, melted

1 teaspoon vanilla extract

1 cup all-purpose flour

1 cup chopped walnuts

DIRECTIONS

1. Preheat oven to 250°F (120°C). Grease an 8x8 inch baking pan.

2. In a large bowl, cream together the butter, brown sugar, and eggs until light and fluffy. Stir in the unsweetened chocolate and vanilla until well blended. Mix in the flour, and then the walnuts. Spread batter evenly into the prepared pan.

3. Bake for 1 hour in the preheated oven, or until a toothpick inserted into the center comes out clean. Cool in the pan on a wire rack before cutting into bars.

Chewy Peanut Butter Brownies

Submitted by: **Jo**

Makes: 1 9x9 inch pan

Preparation: 15 minutes

Cooking: 25 minutes

Total: 40 minutes

"These brownies have been a favorite in my family since I was a small child. Because they're so popular, I usually double the recipe. Great with chocolate frosting!"

INGREDIENTS

½ cup peanut butter

⅓ cup margarine, softened

⅔ cup white sugar

½ cup packed brown sugar

2 egg

½ teaspoon vanilla extract

1 cup all-purpose flour

1 teaspoon baking powder

¼ teaspoon salt

DIRECTIONS

1. Preheat oven to 350°F (175°C). Grease a 9x9 inch baking pan.

2. In a medium bowl, cream together peanut butter and margarine. Gradually blend in the brown sugar, white sugar, eggs, and vanilla; mix until fluffy. Combine flour, baking powder, and salt; stir into the peanut butter mixture until well blended.

3. Bake for 30 to 35 minutes in preheated oven, or until the top springs back when touched. Cool, and cut into 16 squares.

Michelle's Peanut Butter Marbled Brownies

Submitted by: **Michelle Roy**

Makes: 1 - 9x13 inch pan

Preparation: 20 minutes

Cooking: 40 minutes

Total: 1 hour

"These brownies are mouth-wateringly rich and combine two of the most delicious flavors in the world - chocolate and peanut butter!"

INGREDIENTS

2 (3 ounce) packages cream cheese, softened

½ cup peanut butter

¼ cup white sugar

1 egg

2 tablespoons milk

1 cup butter or margarine, melted

2 cups white sugar

2 teaspoons vanilla extract

3 eggs

¾ cup unsweetened cocoa powder

1¼ cups all-purpose flour

½ teaspoon baking powder

¼ teaspoon salt

1 cup semisweet chocolate chips

DIRECTIONS

1. Preheat oven to 350°F (175°C). Grease one 9x13 inch baking pan.

2. In a medium bowl, beat cream cheese, peanut butter, ¼ cup white sugar, 1 egg, and milk until smooth. Set aside.

3. In a large bowl, mix together melted butter, 2 cups white sugar, and vanilla. Mix in the remaining 3 eggs one at a time, beating well after each addition. Combine flour, cocoa, baking powder, and salt; mix into the batter. Stir in chocolate chips.

4. Remove 1 cup of the chocolate batter. Spread the remaining batter into the prepared pan. Spread the peanut butter filling over the top. Drop the reserved chocolate batter by teaspoonful over the filling. Using a knife, gently swirl through the top layers for a marbled effect.

5. Bake in preheated oven for 35 to 40 minutes, or until a wooden toothpick inserted near the center comes out almost clean. Cool completely, then cut into bars.

Cassie's Zucchini Brownies

Submitted by: **Cassie**

Makes: 1 - 10x15 inch pan

Preparation: 25 minutes

Cooking: 20 minutes

Total: 45 minutes

"A must for all brownie lovers! These moist brownies are the perfect way to use extra zucchini."

INGREDIENTS

2 cups all-purpose flour

1 teaspoon salt

1½ teaspoons baking soda

⅓ cup unsweetened cocoa powder

1 cup white sugar

2 eggs

2 cups grated zucchini

½ cup vegetable oil

1 teaspoon vanilla extract

½ cup chopped walnuts

DIRECTIONS

1. Preheat oven to 350°F (175°C). Grease a 10x15 inch jellyroll pan.

2. In a large mixing bowl, sift together flour, salt, soda, cocoa, and sugar. Combine eggs, zucchini, oil, and vanilla; blend into dry ingredients. Stir in walnuts.

3. Bake for 20 minutes in preheated oven. Cool in the pan, and then cut into bars.

Can't Tell They're Low-fat Brownies

Submitted by: **Roberta Tripp**

Makes: 1 - 8x8 inch pan

Preparation: 10 minutes

Cooking: 30 minutes

Total: 40 minutes

"This was my attempt to make my mom's brownie recipe lower in fat. My family loves them!"

INGREDIENTS

½ cup all-purpose flour

6 tablespoons unsweetened cocoa powder

1 cup white sugar

⅛ teaspoon salt

2 tablespoons vegetable oil

½ teaspoon vanilla extract

1 (4 ounce) jar pureed prunes baby food

2 eggs

DIRECTIONS

1. Preheat oven to 350°F (175°C). Grease an 8x8 inch square pan.

2. In a medium bowl, stir together flour, cocoa, sugar, and salt. Pour in oil, vanilla, prunes, and eggs. Mix until everything is well blended. Spread the batter evenly into the prepared pan.

3. Bake for 30 minutes in the preheated oven, or until top is shiny and a toothpick inserted into the center comes out clean.

S'more Brownies

Submitted by: **Liza Louise**

Makes: 1 - 9x13 inch pan

Preparation: 15 minutes

Cooking: 30 minutes

Total: 45 minutes

"Delicious! I consider myself more of a gourmet cook and thought of this as a great kids recipe, because they are so easy to prepare. Well, surprise, surprise. They are fabulous and everyone raves!"

INGREDIENTS

1 (21.5 ounce) package brownie mix

6 graham crackers

1½ cups miniature marshmallows

8 (1.5 ounce) bars milk chocolate, coarsely chopped

DIRECTIONS

1. Preheat oven to 350°F (175°C). Prepare brownie mix according to package directions. Spread into a greased 9x13 inch pan.

2. In a medium bowl, break graham crackers into 1 inch pieces and toss with miniature marshmallows and milk chocolate. Set s'more mixture aside.

3. Bake brownies for 15 minutes in the preheated oven. Remove, and sprinkle the s'more goodies evenly over the top. Bake for an additional 15 to 20 minutes, or until a toothpick inserted in the center comes out clean. Allow brownies to cool before cutting into squares.

Chocolate Mint Dessert Brownies

Submitted by: **Kim Getchell**

Makes: 1 - 9x13 inch pan

Preparation: 15 minutes

Cooking: 30 minutes

Total: 2 hours 5 minutes

"It's a brownie covered in mint cream topped with chocolate, mmmmmm!"

INGREDIENTS

1 cup white sugar

½ cup butter, softened

4 eggs

1½ cups chocolate syrup

1 cup all-purpose flour

2 cups confectioners' sugar

½ cup butter, softened

2 tablespoons creme de menthe liqueur

6 tablespoons butter

1 cup semisweet chocolate chips

DIRECTIONS

1. Preheat oven to 350°F (175°C). Grease a 9x13 inch baking dish.

2. In a large bowl, cream together 1 cup sugar and ½ cup of softened butter until smooth. Beat in eggs one at a time, then stir in the chocolate syrup. Stir in the flour until just blended. Spread the batter evenly into the prepared pan.

3. Bake for 25 to 30 minutes in the preheated oven, or until top springs back when lightly touched. Cool completely in the pan.

4. In a small bowl, beat the confectioners' sugar, ½ cup butter or margarine and creme de menthe until smooth. Spread evenly over the cooled brownies, then chill until set.

5. In a small bowl over simmering water, or in the microwave, melt the remaining 6 tablespoons of butter and the chocolate chips, stirring occasionally until smooth. Allow to cool slightly, then spread over the top of the mint layer. Cover, and chill for at least 1 hour before cutting into squares.

Cappuccino Brownies

Submitted by: **Mary Beth Davis**

Makes: 4 - 8x8 inch pans

Preparation: 30 minutes

Cooking: 35 minutes

Total: 9 hours 5 minutes

"Great, creamy brownies. Freeze great. Wonderful to give as Christmas presents to teachers and friends."

INGREDIENTS

2 pounds semisweet chocolate chips

¼ cup instant coffee granules

1 cup unsalted butter, softened

2 cups white sugar

8 eggs

3 tablespoons vanilla extract

1 teaspoon ground cinnamon

1 teaspoon salt

2 cups all-purpose flour

DIRECTIONS

1. Preheat the oven to 375°F (190°C). Grease and flour four 8x8 inch baking pans.

2. Place the chocolate chips and the coffee granules in a double boiler over simmering water. Cook over medium heat, stirring occasionally, until melted and smooth. Set aside.

3. In a large bowl, cream the butter and sugar together until light and fluffy. Beat in the eggs two at a time, mixing well after each addition. Stir in vanilla, cinnamon, and salt, then mix in the melted chocolate. Mix in flour until just blended. Divide the batter equally into the prepared pans, and spread smooth.

4. Bake for 35 minutes in preheated oven, or until the edges pull from the sides of the pans. Cool on a wire rack. Cover, and refrigerate for 8 hours. Cut the cold brownies into bars to serve.

Cheesecake Topped Brownies

Submitted by: **Nancy Gervasi**

Makes: 1 - 9x13 inch pan

Preparation: 20 minutes

Cooking: 45 minutes

Total: 1 hour 5 minutes

"This recipe came about purely by luck. A few years back, I had to make a last minute dessert for a party. I had wanted to make cheesecake but I did not have graham cracker crumbs. I did have a package of brownie mix and frosting. They were a hit at the party and I have made them ever since."

INGREDIENTS

1 (21.5 ounce) package brownie mix

1 (8 ounce) package cream cheese, softened

2 tablespoons butter, softened

1 tablespoon cornstarch

1 (14 ounce) can sweetened condensed milk

1 egg

1 teaspoon vanilla extract

1 (16 ounce) container prepared chocolate frosting

DIRECTIONS

1. Preheat oven 350°F (175°C). Grease a 9x13 inch baking pan.

2. Prepare brownie mix according to the directions on the package. Spread into prepared baking pan.

3. In a medium bowl, beat cream cheese, butter and cornstarch until fluffy. Gradually beat in sweetened condensed milk, egg and vanilla until smooth. Pour cream cheese mixture evenly over brownie batter.

4. Bake in preheated oven for 45 minutes, or until top is lightly browned. Allow to cool, spread with frosting, and cut into bars. Store covered in refrigerator, or freeze in a single layer for up to 2 weeks.

The Truly Most Fantastic Chocolate Brownies

Makes: 1 - 9x9 inch pan

Preparation: 15 minutes

Cooking: 35 minutes

Total: 50 minutes

Submitted by: **Sulistyowati**

"You're gonna love the rich chocolate flavor and special chocolate frosting. I think this recipe makes the best chocolate brownie ever! Try them!"

INGREDIENTS

5 (1 ounce) squares unsweetened chocolate

⅔ cup butter

4 teaspoons hot water

2 teaspoons instant coffee granules

3 egg yolks

3 egg

1 cup white sugar

2 teaspoons vanilla extract

2 cups all-purpose flour

1 teaspoon baking powder

2 tablespoons unsweetened cocoa powder

½ cup walnuts, toasted and chopped

3 (1 ounce) squares unsweetened chocolate, chopped

⅓ cup sour milk

1 tablespoon white sugar

1 teaspoon rum (optional)

1 cup walnuts, toasted and chopped

DIRECTIONS

1. Preheat oven to 350°F (175°C). Grease and flour a 9x9 inch square pan.

2. In a double boiler, or in the microwave, melt 5 squares of unsweetened chocolate with ⅔ cup butter. Combine hot water and instant coffee, stir into the melted chocolate. Set aside to cool.

3. In a medium bowl, beat in eggs, egg yolks, and 1 cup sugar until smooth. Stir in vanilla. Sift together flour, baking powder, and cocoa; mix into the egg mixture. Next, mix in the cooled chocolate mixture. Stir in ½ cup walnuts. Spread the batter into the prepared pan.

4. Bake for 30 to 35 minutes in the preheated oven. Cool completely before frosting.

5. To make the frosting, melt the remaining 3 squares of unsweetened chocolate in a double boiler. Stir in sour milk, and 1 tablespoon sugar; stir until smooth. Remove from heat, and stir in the rum. Spread over the cooled brownies, and sprinkle with remaining walnuts. Allow the frosting to set before cutting into bars.

Butter Pecan Bars

Submitted by: **Franci**

Makes: 1 - 8x8 inch pan

Preparation: 15 minutes

Cooking: 40 minutes

Total: 55 minutes

"A friend of mine, who picks pecans every year, brought me some of these yummy bars along with a sack of pecans. They are incredibly rich and gooey, and freeze like a dream. Easy and perfect for the holiday season."

INGREDIENTS

3/4 cup butter, softened

1 cup white sugar

1 cup packed brown sugar

2 eggs

1 teaspoon vanilla extract

1 1/4 cups all-purpose flour

1 cup pecan halves

DIRECTIONS

1. Preheat oven to 350°F (175°C). Grease an 8x8 inch square baking pan.

2. In a medium bowl, cream together the butter, brown sugar, and white sugar. Beat in the eggs and vanilla. Stir in the flour and pecans until just blended. Spread the mixture evenly into the prepared pan.

3. Bake for 35 to 40 minutes in the preheated oven, or until edges begin to pull away from the sides of the pan. Allow bars to cool in the pan before cutting.

Vanilla Brownies

Submitted by: **Stephanie**

Makes: 1 - 10x15 inch pan

Preparation: 15 minutes

Cooking: 45 minutes

Total: 1 hour

"I like to include the chocolate chips because I love chocolate, but they can be omitted. I have made them without the chips and they still came out great!"

INGREDIENTS

2¼ cups all-purpose flour

2½ teaspoons baking powder

½ teaspoon salt

¾ cup unsalted butter, softened

1¼ cups white sugar

1¼ cups packed brown sugar

1 teaspoon vanilla extract

3 eggs

2 cups semisweet chocolate chips (optional)

DIRECTIONS

1. Preheat oven to 350°F (175°C). Grease a 10x15 inch jellyroll pan.

2. In a small bowl, combine flour, baking powder, and salt. Set aside. In a large bowl, cream together the butter, white sugar, brown sugar, and vanilla until smooth. Beat in the eggs, one at a time, then stir in the flour mixture. Mix in chocolate chips, if desired. Spread the batter evenly into the prepared pan.

3. Bake for 35 to 45 minutes in preheated oven. Cool in the pan on a wire rack. When completely cooled, cut into squares.

Bar Cookies from Cake Mix

Submitted by: **Penny**

Makes: 1 - 9x13 inch pan

Preparation: 10 minutes

Cooking: 40 minutes

Total: 50 minutes

"A bar cookie that has chocolate chips and nuts. This is easy and delicious ."

INGREDIENTS

½ cup butter

½ cup packed brown sugar

2 tablespoons water

1 egg

1 (18.25 ounce) package white cake mix

1 cup chopped walnuts

2 cups semisweet chocolate chips

DIRECTIONS

1. Preheat oven to 350°F (175°C). Grease a 9x13 inch baking pan.

2. In a large bowl, cream together the butter and sugar until light and fluffy. Mix in water and egg, then stir in cake mix. Finally, mix in nuts and chocolate chips. Spread mixture into pan.

3. Bake for 30 to 35 minutes in the preheated oven. Cool completely before cutting into bars.

Chocolate Chip Cheesecake Brownies

Submitted by: **Barb W.**

Makes: 1 - 9x13 inch pan

Preparation: 25 minutes

Cooking: 45 minutes

Total: 1 hour 10 minutes

"Here's a scrumptious recipe that combines a blonde brownie and cheesecake!"

INGREDIENTS

1 cup shortening

1 cup brown sugar

½ cup white sugar

1 teaspoon vanilla extract

3 eggs

2 cups all-purpose flour

1 teaspoon baking soda

½ teaspoon salt

1½ cups semisweet chocolate chips

2 (8 ounce) packages cream cheese

¼ cup white sugar

2 eggs

1 cup chopped pecans

DIRECTIONS

1. Preheat the oven to 350°F (175°C). Grease a 9x13 inch pan.

2. In a large bowl, cream together shortening, brown sugar, and ½ cup white sugar. Beat in the 3 eggs one at a time, then stir in the vanilla. Combine the flour, baking soda, and salt; blend into the sugar mixture. Stir in chocolate chips, and set aside.

3. In a separate bowl, mix together the cream cheese and ¼ cup white sugar. Mix in the 2 remaining eggs.

4. Spread ½ of chocolate chip dough in bottom of the prepared pan. Pour cream cheese batter on top of dough. Sprinkle with pecans. Drop pieces of the remaining chocolate chip batter over filling. Don't worry if there are gaps; the batter will spread.

5. Bake for 45 minutes in preheated oven, or until lightly browned on the top. Let the brownies cool in the pan before cutting into bars.

Disappearing Marshmallow Brownies

Submitted by: **Maryl**

Makes: 1 - 9x13 inch pan

Preparation: 20 minutes

Cooking: 20 minutes

Total: 40 minutes

"A chewy blonde brownie. Please pass the milk!"

INGREDIENTS

1/2 cup butter

1 cup butterscotch chips

2/3 cup packed brown sugar

2 eggs

1 teaspoon vanilla extract

1 1/2 cups all-purpose flour

2 teaspoons baking powder

1/2 teaspoon salt

2 cups miniature marshmallows

1 cup semisweet chocolate chips

DIRECTIONS

1. Preheat oven to 350°F (175°C). Grease a 9x13 inch pan.

2. Using a microwave-safe bowl, melt the butterscotch chips and butter together in the microwave, stirring occasionally until smooth. Set aside to cool.

3. In a large bowl, stir together the brown sugar, eggs, and vanilla. Mix in the melted butterscotch chips, then the flour, baking powder, and salt until smooth. Stir in the marshmallows and chocolate chips last. Spread the batter evenly into the prepared baking pan.

4. Bake for 15 to 20 minutes in preheated oven. Cool, and cut into squares.

White Chocolate Blondies

Submitted by: **Jenn Rochon**

Makes: 1 - 9x9 inch pan

Preparation: 20 minutes

Cooking: 25 minutes

Total: 45 minutes

"These bars have become an office favorite — they are naughty but OH SO NICE!"

INGREDIENTS

8 ounces white chocolate, chopped

1 tablespoon vanilla extract

1/2 cup butter, softened

1 1/4 cups all-purpose flour

2 eggs

3/4 teaspoon salt

1/3 cup white sugar

1 cup semisweet chocolate chips

DIRECTIONS

1. Preheat oven to 350°F (175°C). Grease a 9x9 inch baking pan. Melt white chocolate and butter in the top of a double boiler, over barely simmering water. Stir occasionally until smooth. Set aside to cool.

2. In a large bowl, using an electric mixer, beat eggs until foamy. With the mixer still running, gradually add the sugar and vanilla. Drizzle in the melted white chocolate mixture. Combine the flour and salt; fold into the white chocolate mixture using a rubber spatula or wooden spoon. Fold in chocolate chips. Spread the batter evenly into the prepared pan.

3. Bake for 25 minutes in the preheated oven, or until a toothpick inserted in the middle comes out clean. Cool pan on a wire rack before cutting into bars.

Becky's Oatmeal Carmelitas

Submitted by: **Robin J.**

Makes: 1 - 9x13 inch pan

Preparation: 20 minutes

Cooking: 30 minutes

Total: 50 minutes

"A good friend of mine (and one of the best cooks I know) created this delightfully chewy caramel bar."

INGREDIENTS

1 (14 ounce) package individually wrapped caramels, unwrapped

1/2 cup evaporated milk

2 cups all-purpose flour

2 cups quick cooking oats

1 1/2 cups packed brown sugar

1 teaspoon baking soda

1/2 teaspoon salt

1 cup butter, melted

2 cups semisweet chocolate chips

1 cup chopped walnuts

DIRECTIONS

1. Preheat oven to 350°F (175°C). Grease a 9x13 inch baking pan.

2. In a saucepan over medium heat, melt the caramels with the evaporated milk, stirring frequently until smooth. Set aside.

3. In a medium bowl, stir together the flour, oats, brown sugar, baking soda, and salt. Stir in the melted butter. Press half of the mixture into the bottom of the prepared pan.

4. Bake for 10 minutes in the preheated oven. Remove from the oven, and sprinkle the crust with chocolate chips and walnuts. Drizzle the caramel mixture over all. Crumble the remaining oat mixture evenly over the top, and pat down lightly.

5. Bake for an additional 15 to 20 minutes, or until the top is golden. Cool before cutting into bars.

Granola Bars III

Submitted by: **Ilene**

Makes: 1 - 9x13 inch pan

Preparation: 15 minutes

Cooking: 25 minutes

Total: 40 minutes

"Absolutely delicious! Granola bars with honey, nuts and raisins. These make a great snack!"

INGREDIENTS

2 cups quick cooking oats

1 cup all-purpose flour

3/4 cup packed brown sugar

3/4 cup raisins

1/2 cup wheat germ

1/2 teaspoon salt

1/2 teaspoon ground cinnamon

1/2 cup chopped English walnuts

1/2 cup vegetable oil

1/2 cup honey

1 egg

2 teaspoons vanilla extract

DIRECTIONS

1. Preheat oven to 350°F (175°C). Line a 9x13 inch baking pan with aluminum foil or parchment paper, and spray with vegetable oil spray.

2. In a large bowl, stir together oats, flour, brown sugar, raisins, wheat germ, salt, cinnamon, and walnuts. In a smaller bowl, thoroughly blend oil, honey, egg, and vanilla; pour into the flour mixture, and mix by hand until the liquid is evenly distributed. Press evenly into the prepared baking pan.

3. Bake 25 to 30 minutes in the preheated oven, or until the edges are golden. Cool completely in pan before turning out onto a cutting board and cutting into bars.

Chocolate Revel Bars

Submitted by: **Holly**

Makes: 1 - 9x13 inch pan
Preparation: 30 minutes
Cooking: 35 minutes
Total: 1 hour 5 minutes

"Chewy, bar type cookies loaded with fudgy filling. A family favorite."

INGREDIENTS

3 cups quick cooking oats

2½ cups all-purpose flour

1 teaspoon baking soda

1 teaspoon salt

1 cup butter, softened

2 cups packed brown sugar

2 eggs

4 teaspoons vanilla extract

1 (14 ounce) can sweetened condensed milk

1½ cups semisweet chocolate chips

2 tablespoons butter

½ teaspoon salt

½ cup chopped walnuts

DIRECTIONS

1. Preheat oven to 350°F (175°C). Lightly grease a 9x13 inch baking pan.

2. In a large bowl, beat together 1 cup butter and brown sugar until fluffy. Mix in eggs and 2 teaspoons vanilla. In another bowl, combine oats, flour, baking soda, and 1 teaspoon salt; stir into butter mixture. Set aside.

3. In a medium saucepan, heat sweetened condensed milk, chocolate chips, 2 tablespoons butter, and ½ teaspoon salt over low heat, stirring until smooth. Remove from heat. Stir in walnuts and 2 teaspoons vanilla.

4. Pat ⅔ of the oat mixture into the bottom of the prepared pan. Spread chocolate mixture evenly over the top, and dot with remaining oat mixture.

5. Bake for 30 to 35 minutes in preheated oven. Let cool on a wire rack, then cut into bars.

Nanaimo Bars II

Submitted by: **Shirly M**

Makes: 1 - 9x9 inch pan
Preparation: 30 minutes
Cooking: 10 minutes
Total: 7 hours 10 minutes

"A no-bake square, that freezes well. I make these during the year, but they are a must on my Christmas baking list as family and friends look for them. My parents live just outside of Nanaimo, B.C. Canada."

INGREDIENTS

½ cup butter

2 (1 ounce) squares semisweet chocolate

⅓ cup white sugar

1 pasteurized egg, beaten

1 cup rolled oats

1½ cups flaked coconut

½ cup chopped walnuts

1 teaspoon vanilla extract

2 cups confectioners' sugar

3 tablespoons butter, softened

½ teaspoon vanilla extract

2½ tablespoons milk

1 tablespoon butter

2 (1 ounce) squares semisweet chocolate

DIRECTIONS

1. In a saucepan, melt ½ cup butter or margarine with 2 squares chocolate. Remove from the heat, and stir in white sugar, egg, rolled oats, coconut, chopped nuts, and 1 teaspoon vanilla extract. Press mixture into a greased 9 inch square pan, and chill for 1 hour.

2. Combine confectioners' sugar with 3 tablespoons softened butter, ½ teaspoon of the vanilla, and milk. Mix until it has an icing-like consistency, and spread it over the oat mixture in the pan. Chill for ½ hour.

3. Melt remaining 1 tablespoon butter or margarine with remaining 2 squares chocolate. Spread over the top of the bars. Chill for 4 to 5 hours.

4. Cut into squares using a hot knife; dip knife in hot water, and let it melt through the chocolate.

No Bake Chocolate Oat Bars

Submitted by: **Traci**

Makes: 1 - 9x9 inch pan
Preparation: 30 minutes
Total: 3 hours 30 minutes

"I baked about 100 dozen cookies for the holidays and these were everyone's favorite!! These bars can be frozen, just thaw 10 minutes before serving."

INGREDIENTS

1 cup butter

½ cup packed brown sugar

1 teaspoon vanilla extract

3 cups quick cooking oats

1 cup semisweet chocolate chips

½ cup peanut butter

DIRECTIONS

1. Grease a 9x9 inch square pan.

2. Melt butter in large saucepan over medium heat. Stir in brown sugar and vanilla. Mix in the oats. Cook over low heat 2 to 3 minutes, or until ingredients are well blended. Press half of mixture into the bottom of the prepared pan. Reserve the other half for topping.

3. Meanwhile, melt chocolate chips and peanut butter in a small heavy saucepan over low heat, stirring frequently until smooth. Pour the chocolate mixture over the crust in the pan, and spread evenly with a knife or the back of a spoon.

4. Crumble the remaining oat mixture over the chocolate layer, pressing in gently. Cover, and refrigerate 2 to 3 hours or overnight. Bring to room temperature before cutting into bars.

Chocolate Scotcheroos

Submitted by: **Debbie**

Makes: 1 - 9x13 inch pan

Preparation: 20 minutes

Cooking: 5 minutes

Total: 45 minutes

"A very sweet bar cookie that can be made with Special K™ or crispy rice cereal."

INGREDIENTS

1 cup white sugar

1 cup light corn syrup

1 cup peanut butter

6 cups crispy rice cereal

1 cup semisweet chocolate chips

1 cup butterscotch chips

DIRECTIONS

1. Butter a 9x13 inch baking pan.

2. In a saucepan over medium heat, combine the sugar and corn syrup, and bring to a rolling boil. Remove from heat, and stir in peanut butter. Mix in the rice cereal until evenly coated. Press the mixture into the prepared pan.

3. In a glass bowl in the microwave, melt the chocolate and butterscotch chips, stirring occasionally until smooth and well blended. Spread over the top of the bars. Chill until set, then cut into bars.

Crunchy Fudge Sandwiches

Submitted by: **Lori Saloom**

Makes: 1 - 9x13 inch pan

Preparation: 15 minutes

Cooking: 10 minutes

Total: 1 hour 25 minutes

"This is a sure favorite with children and so easy to make!"

INGREDIENTS

2 cups butterscotch chips

1 cup creamy peanut butter

8 cups crisp rice cereal

2 cups semisweet chocolate chips

4 tablespoons butter or margarine

1 cup confectioners' sugar

2 tablespoons water

DIRECTIONS

1. Butter a 9x13 inch baking dish. In a large saucepan, melt the butterscotch chips with the peanut butter, stirring frequently until smooth. Stir in the crisp rice cereal. Press half of the cereal mixture into the bottom of the prepared pan.

2. In the top of a double boiler, melt chocolate chips and butter together, stirring occasionally. Mix in confectioners' sugar and water, and stir until smooth. Spread the chocolate mixture evenly over the cereal layer in the pan. Top with the remaining cereal mixture, and press down lightly. Cover, and chill for about 1 hour before cutting into squares.

Chocolate Puffed Wheat Squares

Submitted by: **B. J. Rowlinson**

Makes: 1 - 9x9 inch pan

Preparation: 15 minutes

Total: 45 minutes

"MMMMMM... mom, can we have some more? A deliciously chocolaty square that packs well in little one's lunches.. (big one's too!). Enjoy!"

INGREDIENTS

8 cups puffed wheat cereal

3 tablespoons unsweetened cocoa powder

1/3 cup corn syrup

1/4 cup packed brown sugar

1/3 cup butter or margarine

DIRECTIONS

1. Place puffed wheat in a large bowl, and set aside. Grease one 9x9 inch pan.

2. Grease the rim of a medium saucepan to prevent boil-over. Place the cocoa powder, corn syrup, brown sugar, and butter or margarine in the saucepan. Cook over medium heat, stirring often until mixture comes to a full boil. Allow to boil for 1 minute, and then remove from heat.

3. Pour chocolate mixture over puffed wheat, and stir until puffed wheat is evenly coated. Using a buttered spatula, press mixture into the prepared pan. Allow to cool, then cut as desired. Wrap squares individually, or store in an airtight container.

Chocolate Chip Crispies

Submitted by: **Geurin family**

Makes: 1 - 9x13 inch pan

Preparation: 20 minutes

Total: 40 minutes

"Like the crispy rice treats, but with chocolate chips and peanut butter."

INGREDIENTS

1 cup corn syrup

1 cup white sugar

1½ cups peanut butter

8 cups crisp rice cereal

1 cup semisweet chocolate chips

DIRECTIONS

1. Butter a 9x13 inch pan.

2. Pour the sugar, syrup, and peanut butter into a large microwave bowl. Microwave on high until it begins to bubble, two to three minutes. Once the mixture is boiling, remove from the microwave oven, and stir in the cereal and chocolate chips until coated.

3. Pour the mixture into the prepared pan. Wet hands, sling off the excess water, and press down the treats until smoothed. Let cool, and cut into squares.

Caramel Crispy Treats II

Submitted by: **Cheryl Gross**

Makes: 1 - 11x7 inch pan

Preparation: 30 minutes

Total: 1 hour 30 minutes

"This is the BEST gooey crispy rice treat ever. I make it for pot lucks, and I always take the recipe with me. A change from the marshmallow bars!"

INGREDIENTS

4 (2.05 ounce) bars milk chocolate covered caramel and nougat (e.g. Milky Way®)

¾ cup butter or margarine, divided

3 cups crispy rice cereal

1 cup milk chocolate chips

DIRECTIONS

1. In the microwave, or in the top of a double boiler, melt candy bars and ½ cup of butter, stirring occasionally until smooth. Stir in cereal until well blended. Press into a greased 11x7 inch pan.

2. Melt chocolate chips and remaining ¼ cup butter or margarine, stirring until smooth. Remove from heat, and spread over the top of bars. Refrigerate for 1 hour, or until firm; cut into squares.

The Best Lemon Bars

Submitted by: **Patty Schenck**

Makes: 1 - 9x13 inch pan

Preparation: 15 minutes

Cooking: 40 minutes

Total: 55 minutes

"Tart, rich and perfection, all rolled into one! Wow your friends with this simple recipe. Hint: No Substitutions!"

INGREDIENTS

1 cup butter, softened

½ cup white sugar

2 cups all-purpose flour

4 eggs

1½ cups white sugar

4 tablespoons all-purpose flour

2 lemons, juiced

DIRECTIONS

1. Preheat oven to 350°F (175°C).

2. In a medium bowl, blend together softened butter, 2 cups flour and ½ cup sugar. Press into the bottom of an ungreased 9x13 inch pan.

3. Bake for 15 to 20 minutes in the preheated oven, or until firm and golden. In another bowl, whisk together the remaining 1/12 cups sugar and 1/4 cup flour. Whisk in the eggs and lemon juice. Pour over the baked crust.

4. Bake for an additional 20 minutes in the preheated oven. The bars will firm up as they cool. For a festive tray, make another pan using limes instead of lemons and adding a drop of green food coloring to give a very pale green. After both pans have cooled, cut into uniform 2 inch squares and arrange in a checker board fashion.

Bake Sale Lemon Bars

Submitted by: **Elaine**

Makes: 1 - 9x13 inch pan

Preparation: 15 minutes

Cooking: 45 minutes

Total: 1 hour

"They are very, very easy to make, and really fabulously delicious."

INGREDIENTS

1½ cups all-purpose flour

⅔ cup confectioners' sugar

¾ cup butter or margarine, softened

3 eggs

1½ cups white sugar

3 tablespoons all-purpose flour

¼ cup lemon juice

⅓ cup confectioners' sugar for decoration

DIRECTIONS

1. Preheat the oven to 375°F (190°C). Grease a 9x13 inch baking pan.

2. Combine the flour, ⅔ cup confectioners' sugar, and butter. Pat dough into prepared pan.

3. Bake for 20 minutes in the preheated oven, until slightly golden. While the crust is baking, whisk together eggs, white sugar, flour, and lemon juice until frothy. Pour this lemon mixture over the hot crust.

4. Return to the preheated oven for an additional 20 to 25 minutes, or until light golden brown. Cool on a wire rack. Dust the top with confectioners' sugar. Cut into squares.

Easy Lemon Bars

Submitted by: **Peggy**

Makes: 1 - 9x13 inch pan

Preparation: 20 minutes

Cooking: 30 minutes

Total: 50 minutes

"These bars are great and easy to make. Hope you like them!"

INGREDIENTS

1 (18.25 ounce) package lemon cake mix with pudding

1 egg

½ cup vegetable oil

1 (8 ounce) package cream cheese

⅓ cup white sugar

1 tablespoon lemon juice

DIRECTIONS

1. Preheat oven to 350°F (175°C).

2. Pour cake mix into a large bowl. Add the egg and oil; mix until well blended. Mixture will be slightly dry. Reserve one cup for the topping, and pat the rest into an ungreased 9x13 inch pan.

3. Bake for 15 minutes in the preheated oven. Set aside to cool. Meanwhile, in a medium bowl, beat the cream cheese with the sugar and lemon juice until smooth. Spread the mixture evenly over the baked crust. Crumble the reserved cake mix mixture over the top.

4. Bake for an additional 15 minutes in the preheated oven, or until filling is set and the topping is lightly toasted. Cool before cutting into bars. Refrigerate leftovers.

Blueberry Crumb Bars

Submitted by: **A. Beavers**

Makes: 1 - 9x13 inch pan

Preparation: 15 minutes

Cooking: 45 minutes

Total: 1 hour

"Cheap and easy to make. Kids love them. Any berry can be used."

INGREDIENTS

1 cup white sugar

1 teaspoon baking powder

3 cups all-purpose flour

1 cup shortening

1 egg

¼ teaspoon salt (optional)

1 pinch ground cinnamon (optional)

4 cups fresh blueberries

½ cup white sugar

3 teaspoons cornstarch

DIRECTIONS

1. Preheat the oven to 375°F (190°C). Grease a 9x13 inch pan.

2. In a medium bowl, stir together 1 cup sugar, 3 cups flour, and baking powder. Mix in salt and cinnamon, if desired. Use a fork or pastry cutter to blend in the shortening and egg. Dough will be crumbly. Pat half of dough into the prepared pan.

3. In another bowl, stir together the sugar and cornstarch. Gently mix in the blueberries. Sprinkle the blueberry mixture evenly over the crust. Crumble remaining dough over the berry layer.

4. Bake in preheated oven for 45 minutes, or until top is slightly brown. Cool completely before cutting into squares.

Cherry Squares

Submitted by: **Karen**

Makes: 1 - 9x9 inch pan

Preparation: 20 minutes

Cooking: 40 minutes

Total: 1 hour 15 minutes

"This sumptuous layered bar cookie is iced with cherry frosting. Cut them small to make bite size morsels that melt in your mouth. You may want to double the frosting recipe."

INGREDIENTS

1¼ cups all-purpose flour

⅓ cup packed brown sugar

½ cup butter or margarine

2 eggs

1¼ cups packed brown sugar

1 tablespoon all-purpose flour

½ teaspoon baking powder

⅛ teaspoon salt

1 cup flaked coconut

½ cup chopped walnuts

½ cup maraschino cherries, chopped

1 cup confectioners' sugar

2 tablespoons butter

½ teaspoon vanilla extract

1 tablespoon water

DIRECTIONS

1. Preheat oven to 350°F (175°C).

2. In a medium bowl, stir together 1¼ cup flour and ⅓ cup brown sugar. Rub in ½ cup butter using your hands or a pastry blender. Press into an ungreased 9 inch square pan.

3. Bake for 15 minutes in the preheated oven, or until lightly browned at the edges. Set aside. In a medium bowl, beat eggs until light. Mix together the brown sugar, flour, baking powder, and salt; stir into the eggs. Mix in the coconut, nuts, and cherries; spread the batter evenly over the baked crust.

4. Return to the oven, and bake for 25 minutes, or until brown. Set aside to cool. In a small bowl, mix the confectioners' sugar, 2 tablespoons butter, vanilla, and water until smooth. Add more liquid if necessary to make a more spreadable mixture. Spread over cooled bars before cutting into squares.

Delicious Raspberry Oatmeal Cookie Bars

Submitted by: **Holly**

Makes: 1 - 8x8 inch pan

Preparation: 15 minutes

Cooking: 40 minutes

Total: 55 minutes

"One of my favorite cookie bar recipes."

INGREDIENTS

½ cup packed light brown sugar

1 cup all-purpose flour

¼ teaspoon baking soda

⅛ teaspoon salt

1 cup rolled oats

½ cup butter, softened

¾ cup seedless raspberry jam

DIRECTIONS

1. Preheat oven to 350°F (175°C). Grease one 8 inch square pan, and line with greased foil.

2. Combine brown sugar, flour, baking soda, salt, and rolled oats. Rub in the butter using your hands or a pastry blender to form a crumbly mixture. Press 2 cups of the mixture into the bottom of the prepared pan. Spread the jam to within ¼ inch of the edge. Sprinkle the remaining crumb mixture over the top, and lightly press it into the jam.

3. Bake for 35 to 40 minutes in preheated oven, or until lightly browned. Allow to cool before cutting into bars.

Raspberry Oatmeal Bars

Submitted by: **Megan**

"Quick and easy, but they taste so decadent."

INGREDIENTS

1 (18.5 ounce) package yellow cake mix

2½ cups quick cooking oats

¾ cup margarine, melted

1 cup raspberry jam

1 tablespoon water

DIRECTIONS

1. Preheat the oven to 375°F (190°C). Grease a 9x13 inch pan.

2. In a large bowl, mix together oats, cake mix, and melted margarine so that it makes nice clumps and there is no dry mix left. Press ½ of the oats mixture evenly into the bottom the prepared pan. In a separate bowl, mix jam with water, and spread over the crust. Sprinkle the remaining oat mixture evenly over the top.

3. Bake in the preheated oven for 18 to 23 minutes, or until the top is lightly browned. Cool before cutting into bars.

Apricot-Coconut Squares

Submitted by: **Jo Whattam**

Makes: 1 - 9x13 inch pan

Preparation: 20 minutes

Cooking: 45 minutes

Total: 1 hour 5 minutes

"The yummiest apricot-coconut squares you've ever tasted!"

INGREDIENTS

1/2 cup butter, softened

1/4 cup white sugar

1 cup all-purpose flour

2/3 cup dried apricots

1 cup water

2 eggs

1 cup packed light brown sugar

1/3 cup all-purpose flour

1/2 teaspoon baking powder

1/4 teaspoon salt

1 teaspoon vanilla extract

1 teaspoon lemon juice

1 cup chopped walnuts

3/4 cup flaked coconut (optional)

1/3 cup confectioners' sugar for decoration

DIRECTIONS

1. Preheat the oven to 325°F (165°C). In a medium bowl, mix together butter, sugar, and 1 cup flour. Press into the bottom of an ungreased 9x13 inch pan.

2. Bake for 25 minutes in preheated oven. In small saucepan, bring apricots and water to a boil, and cook for 10 minutes. Drain, chop, and set aside to cool.

3. In a medium bowl, beat eggs and brown sugar. Stir in 1/3 cup flour, baking powder, salt, vanilla, and lemon juice. Fold in nuts and chopped apricots. Stir in coconut, if desired. Pour over the prepared crust.

4. Bake for an additional 20 minutes in the preheated oven, or until firm. Cool, and dust with confectioners' sugar before cutting into squares.

Apple Squares

Submitted by: **BarbiAnn**

Makes: 1 - 9x9 inch pan

Preparation: 25 minutes

Cooking: 30 minutes

Total: 55 minutes

"Apples, nuts and cinnamon make these bars delicious. They hardly last a day at my house!"

INGREDIENTS

1 cup sifted all-purpose flour

1 teaspoon baking powder

¼ teaspoon salt

¼ teaspoon ground cinnamon

¼ cup butter or margarine, melted

½ cup packed brown sugar

½ cup white sugar

1 egg

1 teaspoon vanilla extract

½ cup chopped apple

½ cup finely chopped walnuts

2 tablespoons white sugar

2 teaspoons ground cinnamon

DIRECTIONS

1. Preheat oven to 350°F (175°C). Grease a 9x9 inch pan. Sift together flour, baking powder, salt, and ¼ teaspoon of cinnamon; set aside.

2. In a large bowl, mix together melted butter, brown sugar, and ½ cup of white sugar with a wooden spoon until smooth. Stir in the egg and vanilla. Blend in the flour mixture until just combined, then stir in the apples and walnuts. Spread the mixture evenly into the prepared pan. In a cup or small bowl, stir together the remaining cinnamon and sugar; sprinkle over the top of the bars.

3. Bake for 25 to 30 minutes in preheated oven; finished bars should spring back when lightly touched. Cool in the pan, and cut into squares.

Paul's Pumpkin Bars

Submitted by: **Deb Martin**

Makes: 2 dozen

Preparation: 15 minutes

Cooking: 30 minutes

Total: 45 minutes

"These are very moist, and so far I haven't found anyone who doesn't love them!"

INGREDIENTS

4 eggs

1²/₃ cups white sugar

1 cup vegetable oil

1 (15 ounce) can pumpkin puree

2 cups all-purpose flour

2 teaspoons baking powder

1 teaspoon baking soda

2 teaspoons ground cinnamon

1 teaspoon salt

1 (3 ounce) package cream cheese, softened

¹/₂ cup butter, softened

1 teaspoon vanilla extract

2 cups sifted confectioners' sugar

DIRECTIONS

1. Preheat oven to 350°F (175°C).

2. In a medium bowl, mix the eggs, sugar, oil, and pumpkin with an electric mixer until light and fluffy. Sift together the flour, baking powder, baking soda, cinnamon and salt. Stir into the pumpkin mixture until thoroughly combined.

3. Spread the batter evenly into an ungreased 10x15 inch jellyroll pan. Bake for 25 to 30 minutes in preheated oven. Cool before frosting.

4. To make the frosting, cream together the cream cheese and butter. Stir in vanilla. Add confectioners' sugar a little at a time, beating until mixture is smooth. Spread evenly on top of the cooled bars. Cut into squares.

Gramma's Date Squares

Submitted by: **Michelle**

Makes: 1 -9x9 inch pan

Preparation: 25 minutes

Cooking: 25 minutes

Total: 50 minutes

"A date filled bar with a chewy oatmeal crust. This is my grandmother's recipe which my whole family loves. You can use almond extract instead of lemon, if you wish."

INGREDIENTS

1½ cups rolled oats

1½ cups sifted pastry flour

¼ teaspoon salt

¾ teaspoon baking soda

1 cup packed brown sugar

¾ cup butter, softened

¾ pound pitted dates, diced

1 cup water

⅓ cup packed brown sugar

1 teaspoon lemon juice

DIRECTIONS

1. Preheat oven to 350°F (175°C).

2. In a large bowl, combine oats, pastry flour, salt, 1 cup brown sugar, and baking soda. Mix in the butter until crumbly. Press half of the mixture into the bottom of a 9 inch square baking pan.

3. In a small saucepan over medium heat, combine the dates, water, and ⅓ cup brown sugar. Bring to a boil, and cook until thickened. Stir in lemon juice, and remove from heat. Spread the filling over the base, and pat the remaining crumb mixture on top.

4. Bake for 20 to 25 minutes in preheated oven, or until top is lightly toasted. Cool before cutting into squares.

Zucchini-Coconut Cookie Bars

Submitted by: **Holly**

Makes: 1 - 9x13 inch pan

Preparation: 20 minutes

Cooking: 40 minutes

Total: 1 hour

"Moist, spicy, and nutty, these bars are healthy snack as well as a treat."

INGREDIENTS

- ¾ cup margarine, softened
- ½ cup white sugar
- ½ cup packed brown sugar
- 2 eggs
- 1 teaspoon vanilla extract
- 1¾ cups all-purpose flour
- ½ teaspoon salt
- 1½ teaspoons baking powder
- ¾ cup flaked coconut
- ¾ cup chopped pitted dates
- ¾ cup raisins
- 2 cups grated zucchini
- 1 tablespoon margarine, melted
- 2 tablespoons milk
- 1 teaspoon vanilla extract
- ¼ teaspoon ground cinnamon
- 1 cup confectioners' sugar
- 1 cup finely chopped walnuts

DIRECTIONS

1. Preheat oven to 350°F (175°C). Grease a 9x13 inch baking pan.

2. In a large bowl, cream together the butter, white sugar, and brown sugar. Mix in eggs and 1 teaspoon vanilla until fluffy. Sift together the flour, salt, and baking powder; stir into the creamed mixture. Stir in the coconut, dates, raisins, and zucchini. Spread batter into the prepared pan.

3. Bake in preheated oven for 35 to 40 minutes. To make icing, mix together melted margarine, milk, 1 teaspoon vanilla, cinnamon, and confectioners' sugar. Drizzle icing over the bars while still warm. Sprinkle chopped nuts over icing. Cut into bars when cool.

Easy Layer Bar Cookies

Submitted by: **Denise**

Makes: 1 - 9x13 inch pan

Preparation: 10 minutes

Cooking: 30 minutes

Total: 50 minutes

"Anyone can make these delicious bars, and look like a pro!"

INGREDIENTS

½ cup butter or margarine

1 cup graham cracker crumbs

1½ cups semisweet chocolate chips

1½ cups butterscotch chips

1½ cups flaked coconut

1 cup chopped walnuts

1 (14 ounce) can sweetened condensed milk

DIRECTIONS

1. Preheat oven to 350°F (175°C).

2. Melt the butter or margarine in a 9x13 inch baking pan. Sprinkle the graham cracker crumbs evenly over the butter. Sprinkle on the chocolate chips and butterscotch chips. Cover with the flaked coconut. Sprinkle the walnuts on top of the coconut layer. Finally, pour the condensed milk over everything as evenly as you can.

3. Bake for 30 to 35 minutes in the preheated oven. Cool, and cut into bars.

Chocolate Toffee Crunch Bars

Submitted by: **Pamela and Victoria**

Makes: 1 - 9x13 inch pan

Preparation: 20 minutes

Cooking: 20 minutes

Total: 40 minutes

"The name says it all. Large yield...it's mom's recipe."

INGREDIENTS

2 cups graham cracker crumbs

¼ cup packed brown sugar

⅓ cup butter, melted

½ cup finely chopped walnuts

1 cup semisweet chocolate chips

½ cup packed brown sugar

½ cup butter

DIRECTIONS

1. Preheat oven to 350°F (175°C).

2. In a medium bowl, mix together graham cracker crumbs, ¼ cup brown sugar, and ⅓ cup melted butter. Press into the bottom of an ungreased 9x13 inch pan.

3. Bake for 8 to 10 minutes in preheated oven. In a saucepan, combine ½ cup butter and ½ cup brown sugar. Cook over moderate heat, stirring constantly, until mixture comes to a boil; boil for 1 minute. Pour immediately over baked cookie base.

4. Bake for 10 more minutes. Remove from oven, and sprinkle with chocolate chips. Let stand for 2 to 3 minutes, until chips are shiny and soft. Spread the softened chocolate evenly over the top. Sprinkle with chopped nuts. Cool before cutting into bars.

Buttertart Squares

Submitted by: **Cheryl**

Makes: 1 - 9x9 inch pan
Preparation: 15 minutes
Cooking: 40 minutes
Total: 55 minutes

"Taste just like butter tarts, minus the tart shell. Very easy to make and delicious!"

INGREDIENTS

1 cup all-purpose flour

2 tablespoons brown sugar

1/2 cup butter

2 eggs, beaten

1 1/2 cups packed brown sugar

1/2 cup rolled oats

1/4 teaspoon salt

1/2 teaspoon baking powder

1 teaspoon vanilla extract

1/2 cup raisins (optional)

1/4 cup flaked coconut (optional)

DIRECTIONS

1. Preheat oven to 350°F (175°C). Butter a 9x9 inch baking pan.

2. In a medium bowl, combine flour and 2 tablespoons brown sugar. Cut in butter until mixture is crumbly. Press into the bottom of the prepared pan.

3. Bake for 15 minutes in preheated oven. Crust should not be fully cooked.

4. In a large bowl, mix together the eggs and remaining brown sugar. Combine the oats, salt, and baking powder; stir into the egg mixture along with the vanilla. Mix in raisins and coconut, if desired. Spread the mixture evenly over the partially baked crumb layer in pan.

5. Bake 20 minutes more. Cool, and cut into squares.

Buttermilk Coconut Bars

Submitted by: **Vanessa**

Makes: 1 - 9x13 inch pan

Preparation: 20 minutes

Cooking: 45 minutes

Total: 1 hour 5 minutes

"One of my favorite recipes...you can't go wrong serving these bars."

INGREDIENTS

1¼ cups white sugar

¾ cup packed brown sugar

2 cups all-purpose flour

½ cup butter, softened

½ cup shredded coconut

½ cup chopped walnuts

1 teaspoon baking soda

½ teaspoon salt

1 teaspoon ground cinnamon

1 egg

1 cup buttermilk

1 teaspoon vanilla extract

1 cup confectioners sugar

1 tablespoon milk

DIRECTIONS

1. Preheat the oven to 350°F (175°C). Grease a 9x13 inch pan.

2. In a medium bowl, combine the sugar, brown sugar, flour, and butter; blend with a pastry blender until the mixture is in coarse crumbs. Remove 2 cups of the mixture to another bowl, and reserve the rest.

3. Stir the coconut and walnuts into the 2 cups of the sugar mixture. Pat firmly into the greased pan. Stir the baking soda, salt, and cinnamon into the reserved mixture. Then mix in the egg, buttermilk and vanilla until well blended. Spread this over the crust in the pan.

4. Bake for 35 to 45 minutes in the preheated oven, or until firm. Allow to cool. Make a glaze using confectioners' sugar and enough of the milk to give it a drizzling consistency. Drizzle over bars before cutting into squares.

Macaroon Cookie Bars

Submitted by: **Elaine**

Makes: 1 - 9x13 inch pan

Preparation: 15 minutes

Cooking: 35 minutes

Total: 50 minutes

"A nice alternative to Coconut Macaroons."

INGREDIENTS

1 (18.25 ounce) package devil's food cake mix

½ cup butter, softened

1 egg

1 (14 ounce) can sweetened condensed milk

1 teaspoon vanilla extract

1 egg

1¼ cups flaked coconut

1 cup chopped pecans

DIRECTIONS

1. Preheat oven to 350°F (175°C). Grease a 9x13 inch pan.

2. In large bowl, mix together the cake mix, butter and 1 egg. Mixture will be crumbly. Press into the prepared pan.

3. In another bowl, mix together the sweetened condensed milk, vanilla and 1 egg until smooth. Stir in 1 cup of the coconut and pecans. Spread the mixture evenly over the prepared crust. Sprinkle remaining ¼ cup coconut over top.

4. Bake for 30 to 35 minutes in the preheated oven, or until golden brown. Cool on a wire rack before cutting into bars.

Peanut Butter Bars

Submitted by: **Nancy**

Makes: 1 - 9x13 inch pan

Preparation: 25 minutes

Total: 1 hour 25 minutes

"These peanut butter bars taste just like peanut butter cups."

INGREDIENTS

1 cup butter or margarine, melted

2 cups graham cracker crumbs

2 cups confectioners' sugar

1 cup peanut butter

1½ cups semisweet chocolate chips

4 tablespoons peanut butter

DIRECTIONS

1. In a medium bowl, mix together the butter or margarine, graham cracker crumbs, confectioners' sugar, and 1 cup peanut butter until well blended. Press evenly into the bottom of an ungreased 9x13 inch pan.

2. In a metal bowl over simmering water, or in the microwave, melt the chocolate chips with the peanut butter, stirring occasionally until smooth. Spread over the prepared crust. Refrigerate for at least one hour before cutting into squares.

Lil' Devils

Submitted by: **Susan**

Makes: 1 - 9x13 inch pan

Preparation: 15 minutes

Cooking: 20 minutes

Total: 35 minutes

"Anyone who loves chocolate and peanut butter together will want to make these easy treats!"

INGREDIENTS

1 (18.25 ounce) package devil's food cake mix

½ cup butter, melted

½ cup creamy peanut butter

1 (7 ounce) jar marshmallow creme

DIRECTIONS

1. Preheat oven to 350°F (175°C).

2. In a medium bowl, mix together cake mix and butter. Set aside 1½ cups of the mixture, and press remainder into the bottom of an ungreased 9x13 inch baking pan. In a medium bowl, stir together peanut butter and marshmallow creme; spread over the crust in the pan. Crumble remaining cake mix mixture over top.

3. Bake 20 minutes in the preheated oven. Cool, and cut into squares to serve.

special occasion cookies

What better way to celebrate a special occasion than with a magnificent array of fanciful cookies? Dainty tea cakes, melt-in-your-mouth meringues, crisp, toasty biscotti — these cookies are guaranteed to impress and delight. Served with fragrant tea, rich dark coffee, ice-cold milk, or a bold burgundy — special cookies are a fabulous finale to any party.

Chocolate Rum Balls

Submitted by: **Donna**

Makes: 4 dozen

Preparation: 45 minutes

Total: 45 minutes

"The holidays will sparkle brightly when you whip up a batch of these chocolate favorites!"

INGREDIENTS

3¼ cups crushed vanilla wafers

¾ cup confectioners' sugar

¼ cup unsweetened cocoa powder

1½ cups chopped walnuts

3 tablespoons light corn syrup

½ cup rum

DIRECTIONS

1. In a large bowl, stir together the crushed vanilla wafers, ¾ cup confectioners' sugar, cocoa, and nuts. Blend in corn syrup and rum.

2. Shape into 1 inch balls, and roll in additional confectioners' sugar. Store in an airtight container for several days to develop the flavor Roll again in confectioners' sugar before serving.

Chocolate Orange Cookies

Submitted by: **Susan**

"Two-colored Christmas cookies."

Makes: 3 dozen
Preparation: 30 minutes
Cooking: 10 minutes
Total: 50 minutes

INGREDIENTS

1 (1 ounce) square unsweetened chocolate

3/4 cup butter

3/4 cup white sugar

1 egg

1 teaspoon vanilla extract

1 1/2 cups all-purpose flour

1 teaspoon baking powder

1 pinch salt

1 tablespoon orange zest

DIRECTIONS

1. Preheat the oven to 350°F (175°C). In a microwave-safe dish, melt the unsweetened chocolate, stirring frequently until smooth. Set aside.

2. In a medium bowl, cream together the butter and sugar until smooth. Beat in the egg and vanilla. Combine the flour, baking powder, and salt; stir into the creamed mixture. Divide dough in two. Mix orange zest into one half, and melted chocolate into the other half. Use a bit of each mixture to form a ball about 1 inch in diameter.

3. Bake for 8 to 10 minutes in the preheated oven, or until center is set. Cool on wire racks.

Acorn Magic Delights

Submitted by: **Lara Braithwaite**

Makes: 3 dozen

Preparation: 25 minutes

Cooking: 12 minutes

Total: 2 hours

"This is an easy yet elegant butter-pecan cookie shaped to resemble an acorn and dipped in melted chocolate chips and chopped pecans."

INGREDIENTS

1 cup butter, melted

3/4 cup packed brown sugar

1 1/2 cups finely chopped pecans

2 1/2 cups all-purpose flour

1/2 teaspoon baking powder

1 cup semisweet chocolate chips

1 teaspoon vanilla extract

DIRECTIONS

1. Preheat oven to 375°F (190°C).

2. In a large bowl, beat together butter, brown sugar, 3/4 cup chopped pecans, and vanilla until well blended. Combine flour and baking powder, and stir into the butter mixture. Shape dough into 1 inch balls, and place onto ungreased cookie sheets. Flatten cookies slightly to keep them from rolling off of the pan, and pinch the tops to a point to resemble acorns.

3. Bake for 10 to 12 minutes in the preheated oven, or until firm. Remove from cookie sheet to cool on wire racks.

4. In the top of a double boiler, melt chocolate chips, stirring frequently until smooth. Remove from heat; keep chocolate warm over water in the double boiler. Dip pointy ends of cooled cookies into melted chocolate, then into the remaining 3/4 cup chopped pecans. Allow cookies to set on waxed paper.

Pistachio Cream Cheese Fingers

Submitted by: **Irene DiCaprio**

Makes: 8 dozen

Preparation: 30 minutes

Cooking: 12 minutes

Total: 1 hour 45 minutes

"These are tender and delicately flavored cookies - the light green color and chocolate drizzle make them stand out on a cookie tray. Nice for holidays or bridal showers."

INGREDIENTS

1 cup butter, softened

1 cup white sugar

1 (8 ounce) package cream cheese, softened

1 egg

1 teaspoon vanilla extract

2¼ cups all-purpose flour

1 (3 ounce) package instant pistachio pudding mix

1 teaspoon baking powder

½ teaspoon salt

3 (1 ounce) squares semisweet chocolate

1 teaspoon shortening

DIRECTIONS

1. In a large bowl, cream together the butter, sugar, and cream cheese until light and fluffy. Beat in the egg and vanilla. Combine the flour, dry pudding mix, baking powder, and salt; stir into the creamed mixture. Cover dough, and refrigerate for at least one hour for easier handling.

2. Preheat oven to 350°F (175°C). Grease cookie sheets. Shape teaspoonfuls of dough into finger shapes, about 1½ inches long. Place cookies on prepared cookie sheets.

3. Bake for 9 to 12 minutes in the preheated oven, or until set and very lightly browned on bottoms. Cool completely on a wire rack.

4. In small saucepan over low heat, melt together chocolate and shortening, stirring constantly until smooth and well blended. Drizzle a small amount of chocolate over each cookie. Allow the chocolate to set before storing.

Butter Cookies II

Submitted by: **Ceil Wallace**

Makes: 3 dozen

Preparation: 15 minutes

Cooking: 10 minutes

Total: 1 hour 40 minutes

"This is a simple butter cookie that can be used in a cookie press, as a drop cookie or made into a roll and sliced. There is no mystery cookie for a cookie press...any stiff butter type can be used. Just be sure to chill it thoroughly so it keeps its shape while baking."

INGREDIENTS

1 cup butter

1 cup white sugar

1 egg

2²/₃ cups all-purpose flour

¼ teaspoon salt

2 teaspoons vanilla extract

DIRECTIONS

1. In a large bowl, cream together the butter and white sugar until light and fluffy. Beat in the egg, then stir in the vanilla. Combine the flour and salt; stir into the sugar mixture. Cover dough, and chill for at least one hour. Chill cookie sheets.

2. Preheat oven to 400°F (200°C). Press dough out onto ungreased, chilled cookie sheets.

3. Bake for 8 to 10 minutes in the preheated oven, or until lightly golden at the edges. Remove from cookie sheets to cool on wire racks.

Cookie Press Shortbread

Submitted by: **Heather**

Makes: 2 dozen

Preparation: 25 minutes

Cooking: 10 minutes

Total: 35 minutes

"This is my mother's recipe and what I use in my Cookie Press/Shooter. It makes delectable little morsels!"

INGREDIENTS

1 cup butter

1½ cups all-purpose flour

½ cup confectioners' sugar

¼ teaspoon vanilla extract

½ cup cornstarch

DIRECTIONS

1. Preheat oven to 350°F (175°C).

2. In a medium mixing bowl, cream together butter, confectioners' sugar, and vanilla until smooth with electric mixer. Stir in flour and cornstarch. Pop dough into your cookie press, and away you go! Press cookies out onto ungreased cookie sheets.

3. Bake for 8 to 10 minutes in the preheated oven, or until the peaks are golden.

Cream Cheese Spritz

Submitted by: **Marge**

Makes: 3 dozen

Preparation: 15 minutes

Cooking: 10 minutes

Total: 40 minutes

"This recipe was given to me many years ago. Try using orange extract for a flavor twist."

INGREDIENTS

½ cup shortening

1 (3 ounce) package cream cheese

⅓ cup white sugar

1 egg yolk

1 teaspoon lemon extract

1½ cups all-purpose flour

½ teaspoon salt

DIRECTIONS

1. Preheat oven to 400°F (200°C).

2. In a medium bowl, cream together shortening, cream cheese, and sugar until light and fluffy. Beat in egg yolk, and lemon extract. Combine flour and salt; gradually mix into the creamed mixture in three additions, mixing well after each. Load dough into a cookie press, and press cookies onto an ungreased cookie sheet.

3. Bake for 8 to 10 minutes in the preheated oven, or until lightly golden. Let cool on the baking sheet for a few minutes before transferring to wire racks to cool completely.

Snow Flakes

Submitted by: **Jessy Davis**

Makes: 6 dozen

Preparation: 20 minutes

Cooking: 10 minutes

Total: 1 hour

"This recipe is for use with a cookie press. Wonderfully soft and more flavorful than the average spritz cookie."

INGREDIENTS

1 cup butter flavored shortening

1 (3 ounce) package cream cheese, softened

1 cup white sugar

1 egg yolk

1 teaspoon vanilla extract

1 teaspoon orange zest

2¹/₂ cups all-purpose flour

¹/₂ teaspoon salt

¹/₄ teaspoon ground cinnamon

DIRECTIONS

1. Preheat oven to 350°F (175°C).

2. In a medium bowl, cream together shortening, cream cheese, and sugar. Beat in egg yolk, vanilla, and orange zest. Continue creaming until light and fluffy. Gradually stir in flour, salt, and cinnamon. Fill the cookie press, and form cookies on ungreased cookie sheet.

3. Bake in preheated oven for 10 to 12 minutes. Remove from cookie sheet, and cool on wire racks.

Butter Snow Flakes

Submitted by: **Linda**

Makes: 6 dozen

Preparation: 15 minutes

Cooking: 15 minutes

Total: 1 hour

"A wonderful Spritz cookie with cinnamon in it. These freeze very well."

INGREDIENTS

2¼ cups all-purpose flour

¼ teaspoon salt

¼ teaspoon ground cinnamon

1 cup butter

1 (3 ounce) package cream cheese, softened

1 cup white sugar

1 egg yolk

1 teaspoon vanilla extract

1 teaspoon orange zest

DIRECTIONS

1. Preheat oven to 350°F (175°C). Sift together the flour, salt, and cinnamon; set aside.

2. In a medium bowl, cream together butter and cream cheese. Add sugar and egg yolk; beat until light and fluffy. Stir in the vanilla and orange zest. Gradually blend in the dry ingredients. Fill a cookie press or pastry bag with dough, and form cookies on an ungreased cookie sheet.

3. Bake for 12 to 15 minutes in the preheated oven, or until the cookies are golden brown on the peaks and on the bottoms. Remove from cookie sheets at once to cool on wire racks.

Raspberry and Almond Shortbread Thumbprints

Makes: 3 dozen

Preparation: 30 minutes

Cooking: 18 minutes

Total: 1 hour 15 minutes

Submitted by: **Dee**

"Shortbread thumbprint cookie filled with raspberry jam, and drizzled with glaze."

INGREDIENTS

1 cup butter, softened

2/3 cup white sugar

1/2 teaspoon almond extract

2 cups all-purpose flour

1/2 cup seedless raspberry jam

1/2 cup confectioners' sugar

3/4 teaspoon almond extract

1 teaspoon milk

DIRECTIONS

1. Preheat oven to 350°F (175°C).

2. In a medium bowl, cream together butter and white sugar until smooth. Mix in ½ teaspoon almond extract. Mix in flour until dough comes together. Roll dough into 1 ½ inch balls, and place on ungreased cookie sheets. Make a small hole in the center of each ball, using your thumb and finger, and fill the hole with preserves.

3. Bake for 14 to 18 minutes in preheated oven, or until lightly browned. Let cool 1 minute on the cookie sheet.

4. In a medium bowl, mix together the confectioners' sugar, ¾ teaspoon almond extract, and milk until smooth. Drizzle lightly over warm cookies.

Cherry Poppyseed Twinks

Submitted by: **Nancy**

Makes: 2¹/₂ dozen

Preparation: 25 minutes

Cooking: 15 minutes

Total: 1 hour

"A great poppy seed version of the thumbprint cookie. These are so good that they are almost addictive."

INGREDIENTS

1 cup butter, softened

1 cup confectioners' sugar

1 egg

1 teaspoon vanilla extract

2 cups all-purpose flour

¹/₂ teaspoon salt

2 tablespoons poppy seeds

¹/₂ cup cherry preserves

DIRECTIONS

1. Preheat oven to 300°F (150°C).

2. Cream together butter and confectioners' sugar until light and fluffy. Beat in egg and vanilla. Mix in flour, salt, and poppy seeds until well blended. Drop dough from a teaspoon onto an ungreased cookie sheet. Make an indention in the middle of each cookie with your finger. If the dough is too sticky, dip your finger in water first. Fill each hole with about ½ teaspoon of cherry preserves.

3. Bake in preheated oven for 20 to 25 minutes, or until edges begin to brown.

Apricot Cream Cheese Thumbprints

Submitted by: **Mellan**

Makes: 7 dozen

Preparation: 15 minutes

Cooking: 15 minutes

Total: 2 hours 30 minutes

"These always look so pretty on the cookie plates I give for Christmas."

INGREDIENTS

1½ cups butter, softened

1½ cups white sugar

1 (8 ounce) package cream cheese, softened

2 eggs

2 tablespoons lemon juice

1½ teaspoons lemon zest

4½ cups all-purpose flour

1½ teaspoons baking powder

1 cup apricot preserves

⅓ cup confectioners' sugar for decoration

DIRECTIONS

1. In a large bowl, cream together the butter, sugar, and cream cheese until smooth. Beat in the eggs one at a time, then stir in the lemon juice and lemon zest. Combine the flour and baking powder; stir into the cream cheese mixture until just combined. Cover, and chill until firm, about 1 hour.

2. Preheat oven to 350°F (175°C). Roll tablespoonfuls of dough into balls, and place them 2 inches apart on ungreased cookie sheets. Using your finger, make an indention in the center of each ball, and fill with ½ teaspoon of apricot preserves.

3. Bake for 15 minutes in the preheated oven, or until edges are golden. Allow cookies to cool on the baking sheets for 2 minutes before removing to wire racks to cool completely. Sprinkle with confectioner's sugar.

Eggnog Thumbprints

Submitted by: **Susan Hollis**

Makes: 4 dozen

Preparation: 20 minutes

Cooking: 12 minutes

Total: 1 hour

"Thumbprint cookies with a delicious filling, these are perfect for Christmas. Does not use eggnog, but they have an eggnog taste. You can substitute 1/4 teaspoon rum extract and 1 tablespoon milk for the rum."

INGREDIENTS

¾ cup butter, softened

½ cup white sugar

¼ cup packed brown sugar

1 egg

½ teaspoon vanilla extract

2 cups all-purpose flour

¼ teaspoon salt

¼ cup butter

1 cup confectioners' sugar

1 tablespoon rum

1 pinch ground nutmeg

DIRECTIONS

1. Preheat the oven to 350°F (175°C).

2. In a medium bowl, cream together ¾ cup butter, white sugar, and brown sugar until smooth. Beat in egg and vanilla. Combine flour and salt; stir into the creamed mixture by hand to form a soft dough. Roll dough into 1 inch balls, and place balls 2 inches apart on ungreased cookie sheets. Make an indention in the center of each cookie using your finger or thumb.

3. Bake for 12 minutes in preheated oven. Cool completely.

4. In a small bowl, mix together ¼ cup butter, confectioners' sugar, and rum. Spoon rounded teaspoonfuls of filling onto cookies. Sprinkle with nutmeg. Let stand until set before storing in an airtight container.

Chocolate Kiss Cookies

Submitted by: **June**

Makes: 3 dozen

Preparation: 20 minutes

Cooking: 12 minutes

Total: 1 hour

"Chocolate kiss filled cookies. A wonderful chocolate treat."

INGREDIENTS

1 cup margarine, softened

1/2 cup white sugar

1 teaspoon vanilla extract

1 3/4 cups all-purpose flour

1 cup finely chopped walnuts

1 (6 ounce) bag milk chocolate candy kisses

1/3 cup confectioners' sugar for decoration

DIRECTIONS

1. In a large bowl, cream margarine with sugar and vanilla until light and fluffy. Mix in flour and walnuts, beating on low speed of an electric mixer until well mixed. Cover, and refrigerate dough for 2 hours, or until firm enough to handle.

2. Preheat oven to 375°F (190°C).

3. Remove wrappers from chocolate kisses. Shape approximately 1 tablespoon of dough around each chocolate kiss; be sure to cover chocolate completely. Place cookies on an ungreased cookie sheet.

4. Bake for 10 to 12 minutes in the preheated oven. While cookies are still warm, roll them in confectioners' sugar.

Peanut Blossoms II

Submitted by: **Rosemarie Magee**

Makes: 7 dozen

Preparation: 30 minutes

Cooking: 12 minutes

Total: 1 hour 30 minutes

"I make these every year for our annual cookie open house. We make about 15 to 20 different kinds of cookies and have a 4 hour open house with friends. We then prepare cookie trays to take to shut ins and freeze the rest to enjoy all year long. My husband helps with this four day project! He's retired ... and I'm partially retired. It has been a long standing tradition that we enjoy every year!"

INGREDIENTS

1 cup shortening

1 cup peanut butter

1 cup packed brown sugar

1 cup white sugar

2 eggs

1/4 cup milk

2 teaspoons vanilla extract

3 1/2 cups all-purpose flour

2 teaspoons baking soda

1 teaspoon salt

1/2 cup white sugar for decoration

2 (9 ounce) bags milk chocolate candy kisses, unwrapped

DIRECTIONS

1. Preheat oven to 375°F (190°C). Grease cookie sheets.

2. In a large bowl, cream together the shortening, peanut butter, brown sugar, and 1 cup white sugar until smooth. Beat in the eggs one at a time, and stir in the milk and vanilla. Combine the flour, baking soda, and salt; stir into the peanut butter mixture until well blended. Shape tablespoonfuls of dough into balls, and roll in remaining white sugar. Place cookies 2 inches apart on the prepared cookie sheets.

3. Bake for 10 to12 minutes in the preheated oven. Remove from oven, and immediately press a chocolate kiss into each cookie. Allow to cool completely; the kiss will harden as it cools.

Farm Macaroons

Submitted by: **Juanita**

Makes: 4 dozen

Preparation: 20 minutes

Cooking: 20 minutes

Total: 50 minutes

"This is a recipe that we made on the farm in the 30's. It is a delicious coconut macaroon."

INGREDIENTS

4 egg whites

1/2 teaspoon vanilla extract

1/4 teaspoon almond extract

1/8 teaspoon cream of tartar

1 1/4 cups white sugar

1/4 cup all-purpose flour

1/4 teaspoon salt

2 1/2 cups flaked coconut

DIRECTIONS

1. Preheat oven to 300°F (150°C). Grease and flour cookie sheet.

2. In a medium bowl, beat egg whites, vanilla extract, almond extract, and cream of tartar until soft peaks form. Gradually beat in sugar, and whip until stiff. Toss together flour, salt, and coconut in a separate bowl; fold into egg whites. Drop by heaping tablespoonfuls onto the prepared cookie sheet.

3. Bake 18 to 20 minutes in the preheated oven, or until slightly golden. Allow cookies to cool on the baking sheet for easy removal.

Macaroons III

Submitted by: **Gayle Marie Larson**

Makes: 5 dozen

Preparation: 15 minutes

Cooking: 12 minutes

Total: 50 minutes

"Simple soft, chewy recipe. You can add a lot of things or... nothing at all. I have never tried them chocolate covered but I am sure this recipe, after cooled, could be dipped in chocolate as well!"

INGREDIENTS

1 (14 ounce) package flaked coconut

1 (14 ounce) can sweetened condensed milk

2 teaspoons vanilla extract

DIRECTIONS

1. Preheat the oven to 350°F (175°C). Grease cookie sheets.

2. In a medium bowl, mix together the coconut, sweetened condensed milk, and vanilla until well blended. Drop by teaspoonfuls, one inch apart, onto the prepared cookie sheets.

3. Bake for 10 to 12 minutes in the preheated oven, or until edges are slightly browned. Using a moistened spatula, remove at once from baking sheets. Cool on cooling racks until firm. Store in a covered container at room temperature.

Pecan Clouds

Submitted by: **Carol Eggers**

"Melt in your mouth pecan cookies."

Makes: 2 dozen

Preparation: 15 minutes

Cooking: 1 hour 30 minutes

Total: 1 hour 45 minutes

INGREDIENTS

2 egg whites

1 teaspoon vanilla extract

3/4 cup packed light brown sugar

2 cups pecan halves

DIRECTIONS

1. Preheat oven to 250°F (120°C). Lightly grease a cookie sheet.

2. In a large glass or metal mixing bowl, beat egg whites to soft peaks. Gradually add sugar, continuing to beat until whites form stiff peaks. Stir in vanilla and pecans. Drop mounded spoonfuls onto the prepared cookie sheet.

3. Bake 1 hour in the preheated oven. Turn off heat, and allow to remain in oven at least another 30 minutes, or until the centers of cookies are dry.

Peppermint Meringues

Submitted by: **Kathy Brandt**

Makes: 4 dozen

Preparation: 20 minutes

Cooking: 1 hour 30 minutes

Total: 5 hours

"These are very good, light and airy. The colors are great for the holidays."

INGREDIENTS

2 egg whites

1/8 teaspoon salt

1/8 teaspoon cream of tartar

1/2 cup white sugar

2 peppermint candy canes, crushed

DIRECTIONS

1. Preheat oven to 225°F (110°C). Line 2 cookie sheets with foil.

2. In a large glass or metal mixing bowl, beat egg whites, salt, and cream of tartar to soft peaks. Gradually add sugar, continuing to beat until whites form stiff peaks. Drop by spoonfuls 1 inch apart on the prepared cookie sheets. Sprinkle crushed peppermint candy over the cookies.

3. Bake for 1½ hours in preheated oven. Meringues should be completely dry on the inside. Do not allow them to brown. Turn off oven. Keep oven door ajar, and let meringues sit in the oven until completely cool. Loosen from foil with metal spatula. Store loosely covered in cool dry place for up to 2 months.

Cinnamon Hazelnut Biscotti

Submitted by: **Kris**

Makes: 30 cookies

Preparation: 25 minutes

Cooking: 40 minutes

Total: 1 hour 35 minutes

"These are delicious with coffee and they smell wonderful!"

INGREDIENTS

¾ cup butter

1 cup white sugar

2 eggs

1½ teaspoons vanilla extract

2½ cups all-purpose flour

1 teaspoon ground cinnamon

¾ teaspoon baking powder

½ teaspoon salt

1 cup hazelnuts

DIRECTIONS

1. Preheat oven to 350°F(175°C). Grease a cookie sheet or line with parchment paper.

2. In a medium bowl, cream together butter and sugar until light and fluffy. Beat in eggs and vanilla. Sift together the flour, cinnamon, baking powder, and salt; mix into the egg mixture. Stir in the hazelnuts. Shape dough into two equal logs approximately 12 inches long. Place logs on baking sheet, and flatten out to about ½ inch thickness.

3. Bake for about 30 minutes in preheated oven, or until edges are golden and the center is firm. Remove from oven to cool on the pans. When loaves are cool enough to handle, use a serrated knife to slice the loaves diagonally into ½ inch thick slices. Return the slices to the baking sheet.

4. Bake for an additional 10 minutes, turning over once. Cool completely, and store in an airtight container at room temperature.

D'Amaretti Biscotti

Submitted by: **Rosina**

Makes: 3 dozen

Preparation: 25 minutes

Cooking: 35 minutes

Total: 2 hours

"Toasted almond and lemon zest biscotti for any occasion. Try these variations: Use 1/2 teaspoon of either vanilla or anise extract instead of the almond extract; substitute chopped filberts for almonds; toss in half a cup of mini semi-sweet chocolate chips."

INGREDIENTS

3¼ cups all-purpose flour

2½ teaspoons baking powder

½ cup butter, softened

1 cup white sugar

3 eggs

2 teaspoons lemon zest

1 teaspoon almond extract

½ cup toasted almonds, finely chopped

1 egg white

DIRECTIONS

1. Preheat oven to 375°F (190°C). Lightly grease baking sheet.

2. Combine flour and baking powder; set aside. In a large bowl, cream together butter and sugar until light and fluffy. Beat in the eggs one at a time, then stir in the lemon zest and almond extract. Stir in the flour mixture until smooth, then stir in the chopped almonds.

3. Divide dough in two. Shape each portion into a loaf about 12 inches long and 2 inches wide. Place loaves onto the cookie sheet about 4 inches apart, and flatten slightly. Beat egg white until foamy, and brush over tops of loaves.

4. Bake 20 to 25 minutes, or until light brown. Cool on baking sheet for about an hour.

5. Preheat oven to 325°F (165°C). Cut baked loaves diagonally into ½ inch thick slices. Lay slices cut side down on the baking sheet.

6. Bake 10 minutes, or until crisp. Cool on wire rack. Make several days before serving. Store in a paper bag to soften slightly. For longer storage place in a sealed container.

Chocolate Dipped Orange Biscotti

Submitted by: **Peg**

Makes: 10 cookies

Preparation: 25 minutes

Cooking: 50 minutes

Total: 1 hour 15 minutes

"A delightful combination of chocolate and orange. A perfect cookie for any occasion."

INGREDIENTS

1 cup all-purpose flour

1/2 cup white sugar

1/4 teaspoon baking powder

1/4 teaspoon baking soda

1/4 teaspoon salt

1 egg

1 egg white

1/2 cup chopped almonds

2 tablespoons orange zest

4 (1 ounce) squares bittersweet chocolate

DIRECTIONS

1. Preheat oven to 350°F (175°C). Grease a cookie sheet.

2. In a medium bowl, stir together flour, sugar, baking powder, baking soda, and salt. Beat in the egg and egg white, then mix in almonds and orange zest. Knead dough by hand until mixture forms a smooth ball.

3. Roll the dough into a log about 10 inches long; place on the prepared cookie sheet. Press down, or roll with a rolling pin, until log is 6 inches wide.

4. Bake for 25 minutes in preheated oven. After baking, cool on a rack. With a serrated knife, cut into 1 inch slices. Place slices, cut side down, back onto the baking sheet.

5. Return them to the oven for an additional 20 to 25 minutes; turning over half way through the baking. Melt the chocolate over a double boiler or in the microwave oven. Allow chocolate to cool but not harden before dipping one side of the biscotti into it. Place cookies on wire racks, chocolate side up, until cool and dry.

Biscotti Toscani

Submitted by: **Thea**

Makes: 3½ dozen

Preparation: 25 minutes

Cooking: 35 minutes

Total: 1 hour 30 minutes

"These twice baked cookies have a delicate flavor, great with vanilla ice-cream, tea, frozen yogurt, or cappuccino."

INGREDIENTS

⅓ cup butter

¾ cup white sugar

2 eggs

1 teaspoon vanilla extract

¼ teaspoon almond extract

2 teaspoons orange zest

2¼ cups all-purpose flour

1½ teaspoons baking powder

⅛ teaspoon ground nutmeg

¼ teaspoon salt

1 cup semisweet chocolate chips

½ cup toasted almond pieces

DIRECTIONS

1. Preheat the oven to 325°F (165°C). Grease and flour a large baking sheet.

2. In a large bowl, cream butter and sugar until light and fluffy. Beat in eggs, vanilla, almond extract, and zest. Combine flour, baking powder, nutmeg, and salt. Stir into the creamed mixture until just blended. Mix in almonds. Divide dough into two pieces. Form into long flat loaves about ½ inch tall and 12 inches long. Place the loaves 2 inches apart on the prepared baking sheet.

3. Bake in preheated oven for 25 minutes, or until a light golden brown. Cool on a wire rack for 5 minutes.

4. With a serrated knife, cut diagonally into slices about ½ inch thick. Lay the slices flat on the baking sheet. Bake for 10 minutes, turning over once. Transfer to a wire rack to cool.

5. Place chocolate chips into a small, microwave-safe bowl. Melt chocolate in the microwave, stirring every 20 to 30 seconds until smooth. Use a spatula to spread chocolate onto one side of each cookie. Let stand at room temperature until set. Store biscotti at room temperature in an airtight container.

Spring Biscotti

Submitted by: **Elizabeth Lampman**

Makes: 2 dozen

Preparation: 25 minutes

Cooking: 45 minutes

Total: 1 hour 30 minutes

"Fresh tasting biscotti with orange zest, dried cranberries, white chocolate, and pistachios. Very light and tasty."

INGREDIENTS

1/4 cup butter

3/4 cup white sugar

1 tablespoon orange zest

1/2 teaspoon vanilla extract

2 eggs

1 egg white

2 cups all-purpose flour

1 1/2 teaspoons baking powder

1/4 teaspoon salt

2 ounces white chocolate, chopped

1/2 cup dried cranberries

1 1/4 cups pistachio nuts

DIRECTIONS

1. In a large bowl, cream together butter, sugar, orange zest, and vanilla with an electric mixer until light and fluffy. Mix in eggs and egg white one at a time, beating well after each addition. Sift together the flour, baking powder, and salt; gradually blend into the creamed mixture using a wooden spoon. Stir in the white chocolate, dried cranberries, and pistachios. Cover, and chill for 30 minutes, or until dough is no longer sticky.

2. Preheat oven to 325°F (165°C). Line a baking sheet with parchment paper.

3. Turn dough out on a lightly floured surface, and divide into halves. Form each half into a flattish log about 12 inches long by 3 inches wide. Arrange logs at least 3 inches apart on baking sheet.

4. Bake for 30 minutes in preheated oven, or until pale gold. Allow logs to cool on the baking sheet until cool enough to handle. On a cutting board, cut logs crosswise on a diagonal into 1 inch thick slices. Arrange on baking sheet.

5. Bake for an additional 15 minutes, or until golden. Transfer biscotti to wire racks, and cool completely. Store in an airtight container at room temperature.

Cranberry Pistachio Biscotti

Submitted by: **Gerry Meyer**

Makes: 3 dozen

Preparation: 25 minutes

Cooking: 45 minutes

Total: 1 hour 20 minutes

"The red and green make a great Christmas cookie. Have used other nuts instead of pistachios with success. If your pistachios are salted, omit the 1/4 teaspoon salt from the recipe."

INGREDIENTS

¼ cup light olive oil

¾ cup white sugar

2 teaspoons vanilla extract

½ teaspoon almond extract

2 eggs

1¾ cups all-purpose flour

¼ teaspoon salt

1 teaspoon baking powder

½ cup dried cranberries

1½ cups pistachio nuts

DIRECTIONS

1. Preheat the oven to 300°F (150°C).

2. In a large bowl, mix together oil and sugar until well blended. Mix in the vanilla and almond extracts, then beat in the eggs. Combine flour, salt, and baking powder; gradually stir into egg mixture. Mix in cranberries and nuts by hand.

3. Divide dough in half. Form two logs (12x2 inches) on a cookie sheet that has been lined with parchment paper. Dough may be sticky; wet hands with cool water to handle dough more easily.

4. Bake for 35 minutes in the preheated oven, or until logs are light brown. Remove from oven, and set aside to cool for 10 minutes. Reduce oven heat to 275°F (135°C).

5. Cut logs on diagonal into ¾ inch thick slices. Lay on sides on parchment covered cookie sheet. Bake approximately 8 to 10 minutes, or until dry; cool.

Chocolate Cherry Biscotti

Submitted by: **Jennifer Wall**

Makes: 3 dozen

Preparation: 25 minutes

Cooking: 40 minutes

Total: 1 hour 15 minutes

"These are one of my favorites. I make them every holiday season. They are great for mailing and keep for weeks!"

INGREDIENTS

½ cup butter, softened

¾ cup white sugar

3 eggs

2 teaspoons almond extract

3 cups all-purpose flour

2 teaspoons baking powder

½ cup chopped candied cherries

½ cup mini semi-sweet chocolate chips

½ cup chopped white chocolate

DIRECTIONS

1. Preheat oven to 350°F (175°C). Grease a large cookie sheet.

2. In a large bowl, cream together the butter and sugar until smooth. Beat in the eggs one at a time, then stir in the almond extract. Combine the flour and baking powder; stir into the creamed mixture until just blended. Mix in candied cherries and mini chocolate chips.

3. With lightly floured hands, shape dough into two 10 inch long loaves. Place rolls 5 inches apart on the prepared cookie sheet; flatten each to 3 inch width.

4. Bake for 20 to 25 minutes, or until set and light golden brown. Cool 10 minutes. Using a serrated knife, cut loaves diagonally into ½ inch slices. Arrange slices cut side down on ungreased cookie sheets.

5. Bake for 8 to 10 minutes, or until bottoms begin to brown. Turn, and bake an additional 5 minutes, or until browned and crisp. Cool completely. Melt white chocolate in the microwave, stirring every 20 to 30 seconds until smooth. Drizzle cookies with melted white chocolate. Store in tightly covered container.

Brownie Biscotti

Submitted by: **Linda Foster**

Makes: 30 cookies

Preparation: 30 minutes

Cooking: 45 minutes

Total: 1 hour 55 minutes

"A chocolate version of an Italian favorite. You can substitute milk for the water in the egg wash, if you wish."

INGREDIENTS

1/3 cup butter, softened

2/3 cup white sugar

2 eggs

1 teaspoon vanilla extract

13/4 cups all-purpose flour

1/3 cup unsweetened cocoa powder

2 teaspoons baking powder

1/2 cup miniature semisweet chocolate chips

1/4 cup chopped walnuts

1 egg yolk, beaten

1 tablespoon water

DIRECTIONS

1. Preheat oven to 375 °F (190°C). Grease baking sheets, or line with parchment paper.

2. In a large bowl, cream together the butter and sugar until smooth. Beat in the eggs one at a time, then stir in the vanilla. Combine the flour, cocoa and baking powder; stir into the creamed mixture until well blended. Dough will be stiff, so mix in the last bit by hand. Mix in the chocolate chips and walnuts.

3. Divide dough into two equal parts. Shape into 9x2x1 inch loaves. Place onto baking sheet 4 inches apart. Brush with mixture of water and yolk.

4. Bake for 20 to 25 minutes in the preheated oven, or until firm. Cool on baking sheet for 30 minutes.

5. Using a serrated knife, slice the loaves diagonally into 1 inch slices. Return the slices to the baking sheet, placing them on their sides. Bake for 10 to 15 minutes on each side, or until dry. Cool completely and store in an airtight container.

Double Chocolate Biscotti

Submitted by: **Janet Allen**

Makes: 3 dozen

Preparation: 25 minutes

Cooking: 40 minutes

Total: 1 hour 20 minutes

"A crisp, not too sweet chocolate cookie. Wonderful with coffee. Stores very well."

INGREDIENTS

½ cup butter, softened

⅔ cup white sugar

¼ cup unsweetened cocoa powder

2 teaspoons baking powder

2 eggs

1¾ cups all-purpose flour

4 (1 ounce) squares white chocolate, chopped

¾ cup semisweet chocolate chips

DIRECTIONS

1. In a large mixing bowl, cream butter and sugar with an electric mixer until light and fluffy. Gradually beat in cocoa and baking powder. Beat for 2 minutes. Beat in the eggs one at a time. Stir in flour by hand. Mix in white chocolate and chocolate chips. Cover dough, and chill for about 10 minutes.

2. Preheat oven to 375°F (190°C). Divide dough into two parts, and roll each part into a 9 inch long log. Place logs on lightly greased cookie sheet, about 4 inches apart. Flatten slightly.

3. Bake for 20 to 25 minutes, or until toothpick inserted in center comes out clean. Cool on cookie sheet for 5 minutes, then carefully transfer to a wire rack to cool for one hour.

4. Cut each loaf into ½ inch wide diagonal slices. Place slices on an ungreased cookie sheet, and bake at 325°F (165°C) for 9 minutes. Turn cookies over, and bake for 7 to 9 minutes. Cool completely, then store in an airtight container.

Russian Tea Cakes

Submitted by: **Odette**

Makes: 3 dozen

Preparation: 20 minutes

Cooking: 12 minutes

Total: 35 minutes

"This is a family recipe that's been made at Christmas time by at least 4 generations. This year will be the first for number 5!!! 'Bubba' brought it with her when she came from Lithuania. I pass it on in the true spirit of this season!"

INGREDIENTS

6 tablespoons confectioners' sugar

2 cups all-purpose flour

1 cup butter

1 cup chopped walnuts

1 teaspoon vanilla extract

1/3 cup confectioners' sugar for decoration

DIRECTIONS

1. Preheat oven to 350°F (175°C).

2. In a medium bowl, cream butter and vanilla until smooth. Combine the 6 tablespoons confectioners' sugar and flour; stir into the butter mixture until just blended. Mix in the chopped walnuts. Roll dough into 1 inch balls, and place them 2 inches apart on an ungreased cookie sheet.

3. Bake for 12 minutes in the preheated oven. When cool, roll in remaining confectioners' sugar. I also like to roll mine in the sugar a second time.

Almond Cookies

Submitted by: **S. Baker**

Makes: 4 dozen

Preparation: 15 minutes

Cooking: 8 minutes

Total: 30 minutes

"An almond lover's cookie!"

INGREDIENTS

½ cup butter, softened

½ cup white sugar

1 egg

1¼ cups all-purpose flour

½ cup ground almonds

2 teaspoons amaretto liqueur

DIRECTIONS

1. Preheat oven to 400°F (200°C).

2. In large bowl, cream together the butter and sugar. Beat in the egg, amaretto, and almonds. Gradually mix in the flour until well blended. Drop by teaspoonfuls 2 inches apart on ungreased cookie sheets.

3. Bake 5 to 8 minutes in the preheated oven, or until cookies are lightly colored.

Pignoli Cookies

Submitted by: **Adele**

Makes: 3 dozen

Preparation: 30 minutes

Cooking: 18 minutes

Total: 1 hour 10 minutes

"They are pleasantly sweet, made with almond paste and pine nuts, but no flour."

INGREDIENTS

12 ounces almond paste

1/2 cup white sugar

1 cup confectioners' sugar

4 egg whites

1 1/2 cups pine nuts

DIRECTIONS

1. Preheat oven to 325°F (165°C). Line 2 cookie sheets with foil; lightly grease foil.

2. Mix almond paste and granulated sugar in food processor until smooth. Add confectioners' sugar and 2 egg whites; process until smooth.

3. Whisk remaining 2 egg whites in small bowl. Place pine nuts on shallow plate. With lightly floured hands roll dough into 1 inch balls. Coat balls in egg whites, shaking off excess, then roll in pine nuts, pressing lightly to stick. Arrange balls on cookie sheets, and flatten slightly to form a 1 1/2 inch round.

4. Bake 15 to 18 minutes in the preheated oven, or until lightly browned. Let stand on cookie sheet 1 minute. Transfer to wire rack to cool.

Pizzelles III

Submitted by: **Marianne Jungels**

Makes: 2 dozen

Preparation: 15 minutes

Cooking: 35 minutes

Total: 50 minutes

"This recipe calls for a batter-like dough and is baked on a pizzelle iron. Powdered sugar adds an elegant touch. In the Italian version, vanilla is replaced by anise. Chocolate may also be used."

INGREDIENTS

3 eggs

3/4 cup white sugar

1/2 cup butter, melted

1 tablespoon vanilla extract

1 3/4 cups all-purpose flour

2 teaspoons baking powder

DIRECTIONS

1. In a large bowl, beat eggs and sugar until thick. Stir in the melted butter and vanilla. Sift together the flour and baking powder, and blend into the batter until smooth.

2. Heat the pizzelle iron, and brush with oil. Drop about one tablespoon of batter onto each circle on the iron. You may need to experiment with the amount of batter and baking time depending on the iron. Bake for 20 to 45 seconds, or until steam is no longer coming out of the iron. Carefully remove cookies from the iron. Cool completely before storing in an airtight container.

3. For chocolate pizzelles, add 1/4 cup cocoa sifted together with flour and baking powder, 1/4 cup more sugar and 1/4 teaspoon more baking powder. I find that for the chocolate mixture, the iron must be well oiled to start and then brush on more as needed.

Italian Wedding Cookies II

Submitted by: **Donna**

Makes: 3 dozen

Preparation: 20 minutes

Cooking: 45 minutes

Total: 2 hours

"This recipe is an old time favorite of ours. All the kids love these and so do we! Hope you get all the nice compliments I do when you make them."

INGREDIENTS

8 ounces almond paste

1½ cups butter, softened

1 cup white sugar

4 eggs

1 teaspoon almond extract

2 cups all-purpose flour

¼ teaspoon salt

5 drops green food coloring

5 drops yellow food coloring

5 drops red food coloring

1 (12 ounce) jar seedless raspberry jam, heated

12 ounces semisweet chocolate, melted

DIRECTIONS

1. Preheat oven to 350°F (175°C).

2. Break almond paste into a large bowl, and beat in butter, sugar, eggs, and almond extract until light and fluffy. Beat in the flour and salt. Split batter into three equal portions, mixing one portion with green food coloring, one with yellow, and one with red. Spread each portion out to ¼ inch thickness into the bottom of an ungreased 9x13 inch baking pan.

3. Bake each layer for 12 to 15 minutes in the preheated oven, until lightly browned. Allow to cool.

4. On a cookie sheet or cutting board, stack the cakes, spreading tops of the first two layers with raspberry jam. Spread melted chocolate over top of the third layer. Chill in the refrigerator 1 hour, or until jam and chocolate are firm. Slice into small rectangles to serve.

Rainbow Cookies

Submitted by: **Penney**

Makes: 8 dozen

Preparation: 45 minutes

Cooking: 10 minutes

Total: 10 hours 30 minutes

"Moist, mellow and full of almond flavor"

INGREDIENTS

8 ounces almond paste

1 cup butter, softened

1 cup white sugar

4 eggs, separated

2 cups all-purpose flour

6 drops red food coloring

6 drops green food coloring

¼ cup seedless red raspberry jam

¼ cup apricot jam

1 cup semisweet chocolate chips, melted

DIRECTIONS

1. Preheat oven to 350°F (175°C). Line three 9x13 inch baking pans with parchment paper.

2. In a large bowl, break apart almond paste with a fork, and cream together with butter, sugar, and egg yolks. When mixture is fluffy and smooth, stir in flour to form a dough. In a small bowl, beat egg whites until soft peaks form. Fold egg whites into the dough. Divide dough into 3 equal portions. Mix one portion with red food coloring, and one with green food coloring. Spread each portion into one of the prepared baking pans.

3. Bake 10 to 12 minutes in the preheated oven, until lightly browned. Carefully remove from pan and parchment paper, and cool completely on wire racks.

4. Place green layer onto a piece of plastic wrap large enough to wrap all three layers. Spread green layer with raspberry jam, and top with uncolored layer. Spread with apricot jam, and top with pink layer. Transfer layers to a baking sheet, and enclose with plastic wrap. Place a heavy pan or cutting board on top of wrapped layers to compress. Chill in the refrigerator 8 hours, or overnight.

5. Remove plastic wrap. Top with melted chocolate chips, and refrigerate 1 hour, or until chocolate is firm. Slice into small squares to serve.

Neapolitan Cookies

Submitted by: **missy**

Makes: 6 dozen

Preparation: 45 minutes

Cooking: 12 minutes

Total: 5 hours 30 minutes

"This cute refrigerator cookie resembles the popular ice cream flavor. There are chocolate, pink and white stripes."

INGREDIENTS

1 cup butter, softened

1½ cups white sugar

1 egg

1 teaspoon vanilla extract

2½ cups all-purpose flour

1½ teaspoons baking powder

½ teaspoon salt

½ teaspoon almond extract

5 drops red food coloring

1 (1 ounce) square unsweetened chocolate, melted

½ cup chopped walnuts

DIRECTIONS

1. In a medium bowl, cream together the butter and sugar. Stir in the eggs and vanilla. Combine the flour, baking powder, and salt; stir into the creamed mixture. Divide dough equally into three small bowls. Add almond extract and red food coloring to one portion; stir until thoroughly mixed. Mix chocolate into second bowl, and walnuts into the third bowl.

2. Line a 9x5 inch loaf pan with waxed paper, and spread almond dough evenly in the bottom of the pan. Spread the walnut dough evenly over the almond layer, and top with chocolate dough layer. Cover layered dough with waxed paper, and place in the refrigerator until firm, about 4 hours.

3. Preheat oven to 350°F (175°C). Turn out chilled dough by inverting pan; peel off waxed paper. With sharp knife, cut dough lengthwise in half. Slice each half of dough crosswise into ¼ inch slices. Place slices on cookie sheet one inch apart.

4. Bake 10 to 12 minutes in the preheated oven, until light brown. Remove to wire racks to cool.

cookie mixes

A wide-mouth canning jar becomes a work of art when
lovingly filled with layers of luscious cookie-making
ingredients. A pretty ribbon and a handcrafted instruction
card make this a perfect gift. Mail it to faraway friends and
family — you'll fill their homes with love ... and the smell
of fresh baked cookies.

Cranberry Hootycreeks

Submitted by: **Susan O'Dell**

Makes: 18 cookies

Preparation: 25 minutes

Total: 25 minutes

"A beautifully festive cookie in a jar recipe. These make great gifts."

INGREDIENTS

⁵/₈ cup all-purpose flour

¹/₂ cup rolled oats

¹/₂ cup all-purpose flour

¹/₂ teaspoon baking soda

¹/₂ teaspoon salt

¹/₃ cup packed brown sugar

¹/₃ cup white sugar

¹/₂ cup dried cranberries

¹/₂ cup white chocolate chips

¹/₂ cup chopped pecans

DIRECTIONS

1. Layer the ingredients in a 1 quart or 1 liter jar, in the order listed.

2. Attach a tag with the following instructions:

CRANBERRY HOOTYCREEKS

1. Preheat oven to 350°F (175°C). Grease a cookie sheet or line with parchment paper.

2. In a medium bowl, beat together ½ cup softened butter, 1 egg and 1 teaspoon of vanilla until fluffy. Add the entire jar of ingredients, and mix together by hand until well blended. Drop by heaping spoonfuls onto the prepared baking sheets.

3. Bake for 8 to 10 minutes, or until edges start to brown. Cool on baking sheets, or remove to cool on wire racks.

allrecipes tried & true cookies | cookie mixes

Cowboy Cookie Mix in a Jar

Submitted by: **Phyllis**

Makes: 3 dozen

Preparation: 25 minutes

Total: 25 minutes

"Cookie mix layered in a jar. They are great for gift-giving or bake sales."

INGREDIENTS

1 1/3 cups rolled oats

1/2 cup packed brown sugar

1/2 cup white sugar

1/2 cup chopped pecans

1 cup semisweet chocolate chips

1 1/3 cups all-purpose flour

1 teaspoon baking powder

1 teaspoon baking soda

1/4 teaspoon salt

DIRECTIONS

1. Layer the ingredients in a 1 quart jar in the order given. Press each layer firmly in place before adding the next layer.

2. Include a card with the following instructions:

   COWBOY COOKIE MIX IN A JAR

   1. Preheat oven to 350°F (175°C). Grease cookie sheets.

   2. In a medium bowl, mix together 1/2 cup melted butter or margarine, 1 egg, and 1 teaspoon of vanilla. Stir in the entire contents of the jar. You may need to use your hands to finish mixing. Shape into walnut sized balls. Place 2 inches apart on prepared cookie sheets.

   3. Bake for 11 to 13 minutes in the preheated oven. Transfer from cookie sheets to cool on wire racks.

Munchy Crunchy Cookies

Submitted by: **Jo Johnson**

Makes: 30 cookies

Preparation: 20 minutes

Total: 20 minutes

"Flavorful cookie mix layered in a jar for unique gift-giving. If this seems like too much for the jar, just press firmly - the cornflakes will crunch down!"

INGREDIENTS

1 cup all-purpose flour

1/2 teaspoon baking powder

3/4 teaspoon baking soda

1/4 teaspoon salt

1/2 cup white sugar

3/4 cup packed brown sugar

1 cup cornflakes cereal

2 tablespoons flaked coconut

3/4 cup semisweet chocolate chips

1 cup rolled oats

DIRECTIONS

1. In a 1 liter jar, mix flour, baking powder, baking soda, and salt. Pack down, and add the remaining ingredients in the following order: sugar, brown sugar, cornflake cereal, coconut, chocolate chips, oatmeal. Pack down after each ingredient.

2. Decorate jar, and attach a label with the following:

    MUNCHY CRUNCHY COOKIES

    1. Preheat oven to 350°F (175°C).

    2. In a large bowl, stir together 1/2 cup melted butter, 1 egg, and 1/4 teaspoon of vanilla. Add entire contents of the jar, and mix well. Roll dough into 2 inch balls, and place onto an ungreased cookie sheet.

    3. Bake for 10 to 12 minutes in preheated oven. Cool on wire racks.

Cookie in a Jar

Submitted by: **Linda**

Makes: 2½ dozen

Preparation: 20 minutes

Total: 20 minutes

"This cookie in a jar mix has a little bit of everything in it. A great gift idea!"

INGREDIENTS

½ cup white chocolate chips

½ cup crispy rice cereal

1½ cups all-purpose flour

¾ teaspoon baking soda

¼ teaspoon baking powder

½ cup packed brown sugar

½ cup semisweet chocolate chips

½ cup rolled oats

½ cup white sugar

DIRECTIONS

1. In a 1 quart jar, layer the ingredients in the order listed. Pack down firmly after each addition.

2. Attach a tag with the following instructions:

   COOKIE IN A JAR

   1. Preheat the oven to 350°F (175°C).

   2. In a large bowl, cream ½ cup margarine until light and fluffy. Mix in 1 egg and 2 tablespoons water. Add the entire contents of the jar, and stir until well blended. Drop by rounded spoonfuls onto an ungreased cookie sheet.

   3. Bake for 10 to 12 minutes in preheated oven. Remove from baking sheets to cool on wire racks.

Cookie Mix in a Jar

Submitted by: **Laura Ashby**

Makes: 4 dozen

Preparation: 20 minutes

Total: 20 minutes

"Contents for a jar that is filled with the makings for chocolate chip cookies. It helps to pack down each layer to make fit!"

INGREDIENTS

1 cup packed brown sugar

1/2 cup white sugar

1 1/2 cups semisweet chocolate chips

2 cups all-purpose flour

1 teaspoon salt

1 teaspoon baking soda

DIRECTIONS

1. Mix the salt and baking soda with the flour, then layer the ingredients into a 1 quart, wide mouth jar. Use scissors to cut a 9 inch-diameter circle from calico. Place over lid, and secure with rubber band. Tie on a raffia or ribbon bow to cover rubber band.

2. Enclose a card with the following mixing and baking directions:

    ### CHOCOLATE CHIP COOKIES

    1. Preheat oven to 375°F (190°C).

    2. In a large bowl, cream 1 cup of unsalted butter or margarine until light and fluffy. Beat in 1 egg and 1 teaspoon of vanilla. Mix in cookie mix. Drop teaspoonfuls of dough, spaced well apart, onto a greased cookie sheet.

    3. Bake for 8 to 10 minutes in preheated oven, or until lightly browned. Cool on wire racks.

Cookie Mix in a Jar III

Submitted by: **Lisa**

Makes: 3 dozen
Preparation: 20 minutes
Total: 20 minutes

"Oatmeal Raisin Spice cookie mix in a jar with tag attached with directions on how to prepare the mix. These make wonderful gifts to give any time of year, and also for wedding favors, hostess gifts, baby showers, or take to a cookie exchange. Make sure to bake some up so people know what they taste like. Store in a cool dry place away from a heat source so condensation and clumping does not occur. Enjoy."

INGREDIENTS

1 cup all-purpose flour

1 teaspoon ground cinnamon

1/2 teaspoon ground nutmeg

1 teaspoon baking soda

1/2 teaspoon salt

3/4 cup raisins

2 cups rolled oats

3/4 cup packed brown sugar

1/2 cup white sugar

DIRECTIONS

1. Mix together flour, ground cinnamon, ground nutmeg, baking soda, and salt. Set aside.

2. Layer ingredients in the following order into a 1 quart, wide mouth canning jar: Flour mixture, raisins, rolled oats, brown sugar, and white sugar. It will be a tight fit, make sure you firmly pack down each layer before adding the next layer.

3. Attach a tag with the following instructions:

   OATMEAL RAISIN SPICE COOKIES

   1. Preheat oven to 350°F (175°C). Line cookie sheets with parchment paper.

   2. Empty jar of cookie mix into large mixing bowl. Use your hands to thoroughly mix.

   3. Mix in ¾ cup butter or margarine, softened. Stir in one slightly beaten egg and 1 teaspoon of vanilla. Mix until completely blended. You will need to finish mixing with your hands. Shape into balls the size of walnuts. Place on a parchment lined cookie sheets 2 inches apart.

   4. Bake for 11 to 13 minutes in preheated oven, or until edges are lightly browned. Cool 5 minutes on cookie sheet. Transfer cookies to wire racks to finish cooling.

Snickerdoodle Mix in a Jar

Submitted by: **Diane**

Makes: 3 dozen

Preparation: 15 minutes

Total: 15 minutes

"Another 'cookie mix in a jar' recipe for the collection."

INGREDIENTS

2³/4 cups all-purpose flour

1/4 teaspoon salt

1 teaspoon baking soda

2 teaspoons cream of tartar

1¹/2 cups white sugar

DIRECTIONS

1. In a large bowl, combine the flour, salt, baking soda, cream of tartar, and sugar. Stir with a whisk, then place into a one quart canning jar.

2. Attach a tag with the following recipe to the jar:

   #### SNICKERDOODLES

   1. Preheat oven to 350°F (175°C).

   2. In a large bowl, cream 1 cup of butter and 2 eggs. Pour in the snickerdoodle mix, and stir until a dough forms. In a small bowl, combine ½ cup of sugar and 1 tablespoon of cinnamon. Roll the dough into 1 inch balls, roll the balls in the cinnamon-sugar mixture, and place 2 inches apart on an ungreased cookie sheet.

   3. Bake for 10 to 15 minutes in the preheated oven. Cookies should be light brown. Cool on wire racks.

Gingerbread Cookie Mix in a Jar

Submitted by: **Staci**

Makes: 1½ dozen

Preparation: 20 minutes

Total: 20 minutes

"Gingerbread Cookie Mix layered in a one quart canning jar. Great Christmas gift. Place a circle of gingerbread fabric between lid and ring and tie a gingerbread man cookie cutter onto jar with ribbon!"

INGREDIENTS

2 cups all-purpose flour

1 teaspoon baking powder

1 teaspoon baking soda

1½ cups all-purpose flour

2 teaspoons ground ginger

1 teaspoon ground cloves

1 teaspoon ground cinnamon

1 teaspoon ground allspice

1 cup packed brown sugar

DIRECTIONS

1. Mix 2 cups of the flour with the baking soda and baking powder. Mix the remaining 1½ cups flour with the ginger, cloves, cinnamon, and allspice. In a 1 quart, wide mouth canning jar, layer the ingredients starting with the flour and baking powder mixture, then the brown sugar, and finally the flour and spice mixture. Pack firmly between layers.

2. Attach a card to the jar with the following directions:

   #### GINGERBREAD COOKIES

   1. Empty contents of jar into a large mixing bowl. Stir to blend together. Mix in ½ cup softened butter or margarine, ¾ cup molasses, and 1 slightly beaten egg. Dough will be very stiff, so you may need to use your hands. Cover, and refrigerate for 1 hour.

   2. Preheat oven to 350°F (175°C).

   3. Roll dough to ¼ inch thick on a lightly floured surface. Cut into shapes with a cookie cutter. Place cookies on a lightly greased cookie sheet about 2 inches apart. 4. Bake for 10 to 12 minutes in preheated oven. Decorate as desired.

Butterscotch Brownies in a Jar

Submitted by: **Jo Johnson**

Makes: 2 dozen

Preparation: 20 minutes

Total: 20 minutes

"A unique mix that's fun to give and receive!"

INGREDIENTS

2 cups all-purpose flour

1½ tablespoons baking powder

¼ teaspoon salt

½ cup flaked coconut

¾ cup chopped pecans

2 cups packed brown sugar

DIRECTIONS

1. To a one liter jar, add flour, baking powder, and salt; stir together, and pack down. Then add and pack down remaining ingredients in this order: coconut, pecans, brown sugar.

2. Attach a label with the following instructions:

BUTTERSCOTCH BROWNIES IN A JAR

1. Preheat oven to 375°F (190°C). Grease a 9x13 inch baking pan.

2. Empty jar of brownie mix into a large mixing bowl; stir to break up lumps. Add ¾ cup softened butter, 2 beaten eggs, and 2 teaspoons of vanilla extract; mix until well blended. Spread batter evenly in the prepared pan.

3. Bake for 25 minutes. Allow to cool in the pan some before cutting into squares.

Brownie Mix in a Jar II

Submitted by: **Lisa**

Makes: 2 dozen

Preparation: 20 minutes

Total: 20 minutes

"Adorable jars with decorative instruction tags are sure to please, and this delicious brownie mix is the perfect gift for any occasion. Have a baked batch handy when giving the jars so that everyone will know they're in for a treat!"

INGREDIENTS

1 1/4 cups all-purpose flour

1 teaspoon baking powder

1 teaspoon salt

2/3 cup unsweetened cocoa powder

2 1/4 cups white sugar

1/2 cup chopped pecans

DIRECTIONS

1. Mix together flour, baking powder, and salt in a quart jar. Layer remaining ingredients in the order listed. Press each layer firmly in place before adding the next layer. NOTE: Be sure to wipe out the inside of the jar with a dry paper towel after adding the cocoa powder, so the other layers will show through the glass.

2. Attach a tag with the following instructions:

    ### BROWNIE MIX IN A JAR

    1. Preheat the oven to 350°F (175°C). Grease and flour a 9x13inch baking pan.

    2. Empty jar of brownie mix into a large mixing bowl, and stir to blend. Mix in ¾ cup melted butter and 4 eggs. Mix thoroughly. Spread batter evenly into prepared baking pan.

    3. Bake for 25 to 30 minutes in preheated oven. Cool completely in pan before cutting into 2 inch squares.

Brownie Mix

Submitted by: **Denise**

Makes: 16 brownies

Preparation: 20 minutes

Total: 20 minutes

"A delicious and moist brownie mix in a jar. These make the perfect gift for any occasion."

INGREDIENTS

1½ cups all-purpose flour

⅓ cup unsweetened cocoa powder

⅓ cup flaked coconut

½ cup semisweet chocolate chips

¾ cup white sugar

⅓ cup chopped pecans

⅔ cup packed brown sugar

DIRECTIONS

1. In a 1 quart or 1 liter jar, layer the ingredients in the order listed. Pack down firmly after each addition.

2. Attach a note with the following instructions:

   BROWNIE MIX

   1. Preheat oven to 350°F (175°C). Grease an 8x8 inch square pan.

   2. In a large bowl, stir together 2 eggs, ⅔ cup oil, and 1 teaspoon vanilla. Stir in the contents of the jar, and mix well. Spread evenly into the prepared pan.

   3. Bake for 25 to 30 minutes in preheated oven, or until a toothpick inserted into the brownies comes out clean. Cool, and cut into squares.

Sand Art Brownies

Submitted by: **Janet**

Makes: 1 - 9x9 inch pan
Preparation: 20 minutes
Total: 20 minutes

"Mix ingredients in a wide mouth quart size jar, just like sand art that kids make today."

INGREDIENTS

5/8 cup all-purpose flour

3/4 teaspoon salt

1/3 cup unsweetened cocoa powder

1/2 cup all-purpose flour

2/3 cup packed brown sugar

2/3 cup white sugar

1/2 cup semisweet chocolate chips

1/2 cup vanilla baking chips

1/2 cup walnuts

DIRECTIONS

1. Mix the 5/8 cup of flour with salt. In a clean, wide mouth 1 quart or 1 liter jar, layer the ingredients in the order given. Starting with the flour and salt mixture, and ending with the walnuts.

2. Attach a decorative tag to the out side of the jar with the following directions:

   SAND ART BROWNIES:

   1. Preheat oven to 350°F (175°C). Grease one 9x9 inch square baking pan.

   2. Pour the contents of the jar into a large bowl, and mix well.

   3. Stir in 1 teaspoon vanilla, 2/3 cup vegetable oil, and 3 eggs. Beat until just combined. 4. Pour the batter into the prepared pan, and bake in the preheated oven for 25 to 30 minutes.

recipe contributors

A. Beavers 204
Adam Mitchell 36
Adele 252
Alice Hoff 69
Amanda Gladden 119
Amy Sacha 151
Angela 42
Angie 170
Ann 30
Anna S. Uhland 149
Ashley Stay 39
B. J. Rowlinson 198
Barb Lawrence 171
Barb W. 188
Barbara (I) 109
Barbara (II) 81
Barbara (III) 97
BarbiAnn 209
Beatrice 106
Bernie 46
Beth 160
Beth Sigworth 111, 161
Bev 47
Bonnie Smith 125
Carl T. Erickson 175
Carla Maenius 130
Carol 131
Carol Eggers 239
Carol Gutt 89
Carol K. 70
Carol P. 23
Carole Zee 139
Cassie 178
Cathy 165
Ceil Wallace 226
Cheryl 215
Cheryl Gross 200
Christina 118
Christina Pierson 85
Cindy 143
Cindy Becker 27
Cindy Carnes 78
Claire Kalpakjian 123
Courtney 33
Crystal 26

Cynthia Escalante 28
Darlene 112
Dawn (I) 108
Dawn (II) 68
Deanna Storz 32
Deb Martin 210
Debbi Borsick 43
Debbie 196
Dee 231
Denise (I) 213
Denise (II) 142
Denise (III) 270
Diana Lawton 141
Diane 266
Diane Abed 62
Donna (I) 254
Donna (II) 222
Donna (III) 58
Dora 44
Dr. Amy 120
Edie Hathaway 134
Elaine (I) 217
Elaine (II) 150, 202
Elizabeth (I) 38
Elizabeth (II) 173
Elizabeth Lampman 245
Ellie Davies 124
Evelyn Brown 63
Franci 185
Gayle Marie Larson 238
Georgie Bowers 91
Gerry Meyer 246
Geurin Family 199
Gina 157
Hazel Fritz 148
Heather (I) 227
Heather (II) 79
Holly (I) 121, 164, 206, 212
Holly (II) 193
Ilene 192
Ingrid 25, 152
Irene DiCaprio 225
Janet 271
Janet Allen 249
Janet Kay 135

Janice Brubaker 101, 156
Janni 102
Jaylor 41
Jenn Rochon 190
Jennifer 61
Jennifer Wall 247
Jennifer Wilton 75
Jessy Davis 229
Jill Saunders 92
Jo 176
Jo Johnson 262, 268
Jo Whattam 208
Joanna Knudsen 137
Juanita 237
Judy 126
Judy Smith 94
June 235
K.Gailbrath 116
Karen (I) 107
Karen (II) 205
Karen Rose 31
Karin Christian 96
Kathleen Dickerson 84
Kathy Bliesner 138
Kathy Brandt 52, 98, 240
Kathylee 90
Kim 155
Kim Getchell 181
Kris 241
Lara Braithwaite 224
Laura and Tammy 128
Laura Ashby 264
Linda (I) 263
Linda (II) 230
Linda Carroll 34, 162
Linda Foster 248
Linda White 132
Linda Whittaker 51
Lisa (I) 35, 265, 269
Lisa (II) 144
Lisa (III) 163
Lisa Lepsy 37
Liza Louise 180
Lois (I) 115
Lois (II) 74

index

credits

the staff at allrecipes

Jennifer Anderson
Kala Anderson
Karen Anderson
Barbara Antonio
Emily Brune
Scotty Carreiro
Sydney Carter
Jeffrey Cummings
Michael DeLashmutt
Kirk Dickinson
Steven Hamilton
Michael Henderlight
Tim Hunt

Richard Kozel
William Marken
Wendy McKay
Elana Miller
Carrie Mills
Bill Moore
Todd Moore
Yann Oehl
Alicia Power
Elizabeth Rogers
Judy St. John
Britt Swearingen
Esmee Williams

thanks

The staff would like to thank the following people whose comments and feedback have made this a better book: Brenda Hunt, David Quinn, Hillary Quinn, Dan Shepherd, and Rebecca Staffel.

treat yourself to more of allrecipes' best-loved recipes!

allrecipes tried and true cookies

Cookie Lovers Unite! In response to overwhelming demand from our community of home cooks and bakers, we've created a must-have cookbook featuring a collection of over 200 of our best-loved cookies — recipes that have earned the highest ratings from cookie lovers of all ages.

Allrecipes "Tried and True Cookies" cookbook features time-tested favorites: including chocolate cookies, chocolate chip cookies, oatmeal cookies, peanut butter cookies, sugar cookies, bar cookies, cookies in a jar and more!

Soft-covered book contains 288 two-color pages, measures 7" x 9", is fully indexed and lies flat when in use.

Please send me ———— copies of Allrecipes Tried and True Cookies: Top 200 Recipes at $19.95 per copy [Washington residents add 8.8% sales tax to your total order]. Make checks payable to: Allrecipes.com

Mail Books to:

Name: _____

Address: _____

City: _____ State: _____ Zip: _____

Send check to: Allrecipes.com, 524 Dexter Ave N., Seattle, WA, 98109

Allow 4-6 weeks for shipping.

To purchase online go to: http://allrecipes.com/tnt/

treat yourself to more of allrecipes' best-loved recipes!

allrecipes tried and true favorites

In response to overwhelming demand from our community of home cooks, we created this must-have everyday and holiday cooking cookbook. Within the pages of "Tried and True Favorites," your find those recipes from our site that have won standing ovations from our community of home cooks and their families — intrepid eaters and picky kids alike.

This cookbook makes an ideal companion to any kitchen: the recipes are easy to make, call for familiar ingredients, and turn out great each time they're prepared. The recipes, organized into eleven sections (from appetizers to main dishes to cakes & candies,) range from traditional family favorites to innovative creations celebrating the creativity of the everyday homecook.

Soft-covered book contains 360 two-color pages, measures 7" x 9", is fully indexed and lies flat when in use.

Please send me _____ copies of Allrecipes Tried and True Favorites: Top 300 Recipes at $25.95 per copy [Washington residents add 8.8% sales tax to your total order]. Make checks payable to: Allrecipes.com

Mail Books to:

Name: _____

Address: _____

City: _____ State: _____ Zip: _____

Send check to: Allrecipes.com, 524 Dexter Ave N., Seattle, WA, 98109

Allow 4-6 weeks for shipping.

To purchase online go to: http://allrecipes.com/tnt/